KNOW YOUR BIBLE

MAP

A Creative Journal

BARBOUR

PUBLISHING

Published by Barbour Publishing, Inc., 1810 Barbour Drive, Uhrichsville, Ohio 44683, www.barbourbooks.com

Our mission is to inspire the world with the life-changing message of the Bible.

Member of the
Evangelical Christian
Publishers Association

Printed in China.

Today's Date: _____

MY PRAYER FOR TODAY: ....

....

MY TAKEAWAY FROM
TODAY'S READING:

....

....

....

....

....

....

*Know
Your Bible:*

God instructs Noah, the
world's only righteous man,
to build a large boat to save
himself, his family, and two
of each kind of animal from
the flood.

READ:
Genesis 7:10–10:32

Today's Date: _____

MY PRAYER FOR TODAY: ....

....

*Know
Your Bible:*

God chooses a childless
man named Abram to begin
a "great nation," promising
to bless all people on earth
through him.

READ:
Genesis 11–14

MY TAKEAWAY FROM
TODAY'S READING:

....

....

....

....

....

....

DAY 5

Today's Date: _____

MY PRAYER FOR TODAY: ....
....
....

Know Your Bible:

God changes Abram's name to Abraham ("father of a multitude"), promising that his ninety-year-old wife, Sarah, will give birth to a son.

READ:
Genesis 15–18

MY TAKEAWAY FROM TODAY'S READING:

....
....
....
....
....
....

DAY 6

Today's Date: _____

MY PRAYER FOR TODAY: ....
....
....

MY TAKEAWAY FROM TODAY'S READING:

....
....
....
....
....
....

Know Your Bible:

Hundred-year-old Abraham and ninety-year-old Sarah become parents of Isaac, whose name means "laughter."

READ:
Genesis 19–21

Today's Date: _____

MY PRAYER FOR TODAY: ....
....
....

MY TAKEAWAY FROM TODAY'S READING:

....
....
....
....
....
....

Know Your Bible:

God commands Abraham to sacrifice Isaac, then stops him at the last moment, saying, "thou hast not withheld thy son, thine only son from me."

READ:
Genesis 22–24

Today's Date: _____

MY PRAYER FOR TODAY: ....
....
....

Know Your Bible:

Abraham dies and God reiterates His promise to Abraham through Isaac and Isaac's second-born son, Jacob.

READ:
Genesis 25–27

MY TAKEAWAY FROM TODAY'S READING:

....
....
....
....
....
....

DAY 9

Today's Date: _____

MY PRAYER FOR TODAY: ....
....
....

Know Your Bible:

God confirms His promise of blessing to Jacob, who falls in love with a cousin, Rebekah. But Jacob is tricked by her father into marrying her sister, Leah, too.

READ:
Genesis 28–29

MY TAKEAWAY FROM TODAY'S READING:
....
....
....
....
....
....

DAY 10

Today's Date: _____

MY PRAYER FOR TODAY: ....
....
....

MY TAKEAWAY FROM TODAY'S READING:
....
....
....
....
....
....

Know Your Bible:

Jacob's two wives and two of their servant girls give birth to eleven sons, who will become leaders of the "tribes of Israel."

READ:
Genesis 30–31

Today's Date: _____

MY PRAYER FOR TODAY: ....

....

MY TAKEAWAY FROM TODAY'S READING:

....

....

....

....

....

....

Know Your Bible:

Jacob meets a mysterious "man" who wrestles him; the man changes Jacob's name to Israel, "for as a prince thou hast power with God and with men, and hast prevailed."

READ:
Genesis 32–34

Today's Date: _____

MY PRAYER FOR TODAY: ....

....

Know Your Bible:

Jacob's favored wife, Rebekah, gives birth to his twelfth son, Benjamin, and dies; Isaac also dies, at age 180.

READ:
Genesis 35–36

MY TAKEAWAY FROM TODAY'S READING:

....

....

....

....

....

....

DAY 13

Today's Date: _____

MY PRAYER FOR TODAY: ....
....
....

Know Your Bible:

Jacob's favorite son, Joseph, is sold into slavery by his jealous older brothers; he endures great hardship in Egypt by holding fast to God, who makes Joseph prosper.

READ:
Genesis 37–39

MY TAKEAWAY FROM TODAY'S READING:

....
....
....
....
....
....

DAY 14

Today's Date: _____

MY PRAYER FOR TODAY: ....
....
....

MY TAKEAWAY FROM TODAY'S READING:

....
....
....
....
....
....

Know Your Bible:

Using his God-given ability to interpret dreams, Joseph predicts a coming famine and tells Pharaoh how to prepare. Joseph is made second in command of all Egypt.

READ:
Genesis 40–41

Today's Date: _____   DAY 15

MY PRAYER FOR TODAY: ....
....
....

MY TAKEAWAY FROM
TODAY'S READING:

....
....
....
....
....
....

Know
Your Bible:

Joseph's brothers, also facing famine in Canaan, arrive in Egypt to buy grain. They unknowingly stand before the man they had sold into slavery.

READ:
Genesis 42–43

Today's Date: _____   DAY 16

MY PRAYER FOR TODAY: ....
....
....

Know
Your Bible:

Joseph tests his brothers' integrity before finally revealing his identity. They are terrified but he speaks kindly to them.

READ:
Genesis 44–45

MY TAKEAWAY FROM
TODAY'S READING:

....
....
....
....
....
....

Today's Date: _____

MY PRAYER FOR TODAY: ....
....
....

Know Your Bible:

Jacob, who had long believed Joseph was dead, arrives in Egypt for a joyful reunion. Jacob's family is allowed to settle in Egypt.

READ:
Genesis 46–48

MY TAKEAWAY FROM TODAY'S READING:

....
....
....
....
....
....

Today's Date: _____

MY PRAYER FOR TODAY: ....
....
....

MY TAKEAWAY FROM TODAY'S READING:

....
....
....
....
....
....

Know Your Bible:

The dying Jacob speaks a blessing over each of his sons, including a messianic prophecy over Judah, and dies at age 110.

READ:
Genesis 49–50

Today's Date: _____ DAY 19

MY PRAYER FOR TODAY: ....
....
....

MY TAKEAWAY FROM TODAY'S READING:

....
....
....
....
....
....

Know Your Bible:

After Joseph dies, Egypt sees the Israelites as a threat and enslaves them. God raises up Moses to be the deliverer of His people.

READ:
Exodus 1–3

Today's Date: _____ DAY 20

MY PRAYER FOR TODAY: ....
....
....

Know Your Bible:

Moses, with the help of his brother Aaron, confronts Pharaoh with God's message: "Let my people go."

READ:
Exodus 4–6

MY TAKEAWAY FROM TODAY'S READING:

....
....
....
....
....
....

DAY 21

Today's Date: _____

MY PRAYER FOR TODAY: ....
....
....

Know Your Bible:

God sends devastating plagues on the people and land of Egypt, but Pharaoh hardens his heart and refuses to let the Israelites leave.

READ:
Exodus 7–9

MY TAKEAWAY FROM TODAY'S READING:

....
....
....
....
....
....

DAY 22

Today's Date: _____

MY PRAYER FOR TODAY: ....
....
....

MY TAKEAWAY FROM TODAY'S READING:

....
....
....
....
....
....

Know Your Bible:

In the last of ten plagues, God kills the firstborn of every family lacking the blood of a sacrificial lamb on its door-posts. God will "pass over" the obedient Hebrews' homes.

READ:
Exodus 10–12

Today's Date: _____   **DAY 23**

MY PRAYER FOR TODAY: ....
....
....

MY TAKEAWAY FROM TODAY'S READING:

....

....

....

....

....

....

Know Your Bible:

On their way out of Egypt, the Israelites are pursued by Pharaoh's army. God parts the Red Sea to provide an escape route, then destroys the Egyptian soldiers.

READ:
Exodus 13–15

Today's Date: _____   **DAY 24**

MY PRAYER FOR TODAY: ....
....
....

Know Your Bible:

Journeying in the wilderness, the Israelites complain of hunger and God provides miraculous food ("manna") and water from a rock.

READ:
Exodus 16–18

MY TAKEAWAY FROM TODAY'S READING:

....

....

....

....

....

....

DAY 25

MY PRAYER FOR TODAY: ....
....
....

Know Your Bible:

God calls Moses up Mount Sinai, giving him the law for the nation of Israel. God's rules are highlighted by the Ten Commandments.

READ:
Exodus 19–20

MY TAKEAWAY FROM TODAY'S READING:
....
....
....
....
....
....

DAY 26

Today's Date: _____

MY PRAYER FOR TODAY: ....
....
....

MY TAKEAWAY FROM TODAY'S READING:
....
....
....
....
....
....

Know Your Bible:

God gives Moses additional laws for Israel, dealing with personal relationships, private property, and national religious observances.

READ:
Exodus 21–23

Today's Date: _____ **DAY 27**

MY PRAYER FOR TODAY: ....
....
....

MY TAKEAWAY FROM TODAY'S READING:

....
....
....
....
....
....

Know Your Bible:

God tells Moses how to build the tabernacle, a tent that will serve as Israel's portable worship center.

READ:
Exodus 24–27

Today's Date: _____ **DAY 28**

MY PRAYER FOR TODAY: ....
....
....

Know Your Bible:

God defines the role and requirements for Israel's priesthood, under the leadership of Aaron and his family.

READ:
Exodus 28–29

MY TAKEAWAY FROM TODAY'S READING:

....
....
....
....
....
....

Today's Date: _____

MY PRAYER FOR TODAY: ....

....

....

Know Your Bible:

God tells Israel to observe the Sabbath day in perpetuity, and sends Moses back down Mount Sinai with two stone tablets of the commandments.

READ:
Exodus 30–31

MY TAKEAWAY FROM TODAY'S READING:

....

....

....

....

....

....

Today's Date: _____

MY PRAYER FOR TODAY: ....

....

....

MY TAKEAWAY FROM TODAY'S READING:

....

....

....

....

....

....

Know Your Bible:

Moses finds the people worshipping a calf idol they had demanded during his absence. God relents from completely destroying the people when Moses intercedes.

READ:
Exodus 32–33

Today's Date: _____ **DAY 31**

MY PRAYER FOR TODAY: ....
....
....

MY TAKEAWAY FROM
TODAY'S READING:

....
....
....
....
....
....

*Know
Your Bible:*

As the Israelites progress
toward their promised land,
God demands that they re-
main separate from the pagan
people already living there.

READ:
Exodus 34–35

Today's Date: _____ **DAY 32**

MY PRAYER FOR TODAY: ....
....
....

*Know
Your Bible:*

Two gifted craftsmen oversee
construction of the tabernacle, Israel's portable worship
center, using materials given
by the people as an offering.

READ:
Exodus 36–38

MY TAKEAWAY FROM
TODAY'S READING:

....
....
....
....
....
....

Today's Date: _____

MY PRAYER FOR TODAY: ....
....
....

Know Your Bible:

God's glory, like a cloud, fills the completed tabernacle. The cloud will lead the Israelites on their journey to the promised land.

READ:
Exodus 39–40

MY TAKEAWAY FROM TODAY'S READING:
....
....
....
....
....
....

Today's Date: _____

MY PRAYER FOR TODAY: ....
....
....

MY TAKEAWAY FROM TODAY'S READING:
....
....
....
....
....
....

Know Your Bible:

Rules for the priestly class, the Levites, are laid out, including the burnt, peace, and sin offerings to God that they will oversee.

READ:
Leviticus 1–4

Today's Date: _____

MY PRAYER FOR TODAY: ....
....
....

MY TAKEAWAY FROM
TODAY'S READING:

....
....
....
....
....
....

*Know
Your Bible:*

Trespass offerings, covering a
wide range of sinful behaviors,
are explained.

READ:
Leviticus 5–7

Today's Date: _____

MY PRAYER FOR TODAY: ....
....
....

*Know
Your Bible:*

Israel's priests are consecrated
and begin their duties; Aaron's
sons Nadab and Abihu lose
their lives for offering an in-
appropriate fire before God.

READ:
Leviticus 8–10

MY TAKEAWAY FROM
TODAY'S READING:

....
....
....
....
....
....

DAY 37

Today's Date: _____

MY PRAYER FOR TODAY: ....
....
....

Know Your Bible:

God describes the types of food the Israelites may eat ("clean") and that must be avoided ("unclean").

READ:
Leviticus 11–12

MY TAKEAWAY FROM TODAY'S READING:
....
....
....
....
....
....
....

DAY 38

Today's Date: _____

MY PRAYER FOR TODAY: ....
....
....

MY TAKEAWAY FROM TODAY'S READING:
....
....
....
....
....
....

Know Your Bible:

God lays out rules for dealing with "leprosy," a term describing various skin diseases.

READ:
Leviticus 13:1–14:32

Today's Date: _____ **DAY 39**

MY PRAYER FOR TODAY: ....
....
....

MY TAKEAWAY FROM
TODAY'S READING:

....
....
....
....
....
....

*Know
Your Bible:*

God describes how the people can be cleansed, physically and ceremonially, from skin diseases.

READ:
Leviticus 14:33–15:33

Today's Date: _____ **DAY 40**

MY PRAYER FOR TODAY: ....
....
....

*Know
Your Bible:*

Rules are provided for the annual national Day of Atonement. Atonement is only accomplished by the shedding of innocent blood.

READ:
Leviticus 16–17

MY TAKEAWAY FROM
TODAY'S READING:

....
....
....
....
....
....

Today's Date: _____

MY PRAYER FOR TODAY: ....
....
....

Know Your Bible:

The Israelites are commanded to maintain sexual purity, to avoid false worship, and to "be holy unto" God.

READ:
Leviticus 18–20

MY TAKEAWAY FROM TODAY'S READING:

....
....
....
....
....
....

Today's Date: _____

MY PRAYER FOR TODAY: ....
....

MY TAKEAWAY FROM TODAY'S READING:

....
....
....
....
....
....

Know Your Bible:

Priests are commanded to maintain a high level of purity, staying away from any corrupting influences.

READ:
Leviticus 21–23

Today's Date: _____

MY PRAYER FOR TODAY: ....
....
....

MY TAKEAWAY FROM TODAY'S READING:

....

....

....

....

....

....

Know Your Bible:

Various rules demand restitution for crimes, the death penalty for blasphemy, and an agricultural sabbath every seventh year, when the land is allowed to rest.

READ:
Leviticus 24–25

Today's Date: _____

MY PRAYER FOR TODAY: ....
....
....

Know Your Bible:

God promises blessings for obedience and punishment for disobedience, and predicts a future scattering of Israel from the land.

READ:
Leviticus 26–27

MY TAKEAWAY FROM TODAY'S READING:

....

....

....

....

....

....

DAY 45

Today's Date: _____

MY PRAYER FOR TODAY: ....
....
....

Know Your Bible:

Fourteen months after leaving Egypt, in the wilderness of Sinai, God tells Moses to count the Israelites—hence the name of this book.

READ:
Numbers 1–2

MY TAKEAWAY FROM TODAY'S READING:

....
....
....
....
....
....

DAY 46

Today's Date: _____

MY PRAYER FOR TODAY: ....
....
....

MY TAKEAWAY FROM TODAY'S READING:

....
....
....
....
....
....

Know Your Bible:

God claims the tribe of Levi as His tabernacle servants, with Aaron's family as priests and other lines managing the affairs of the worship center.

READ:
Numbers 3–4

Today's Date: _____ DAY 47

MY PRAYER FOR TODAY: ....
....
....

MY TAKEAWAY FROM
TODAY'S READING:

....
....
....
....
....
....

*Know
Your Bible:*

God commands His people
to be pure and undefiled, and
outlines a special level of sep-
aration, the Nazarite vow.

READ:
Numbers 5–6

Today's Date: _____ DAY 48

MY PRAYER FOR TODAY: ....
....
....

*Know
Your Bible:*

The tabernacle is dedicated
in a twelve-day celebration
highlighted by the bringing of
gifts by the individual tribes.

READ:
Numbers 7

MY TAKEAWAY FROM
TODAY'S READING:

....
....
....
....
....
....

DAY 49

Today's Date: _____

MY PRAYER FOR TODAY: ....
....
....

Know Your Bible:

The people of Israel hold their first Passover commemoration after leaving Egypt; the cloud of God's presence leads them out of the Sinai wilderness.

READ:
Numbers 8–10

MY TAKEAWAY FROM TODAY'S READING:
....
....
....
....
....
....

DAY 50

Today's Date: _____

MY PRAYER FOR TODAY: ....
....
....

MY TAKEAWAY FROM TODAY'S READING:
....
....
....
....
....
....

Know Your Bible:

The people soon complain about God's manna, bringing judgment on themselves; even Moses' siblings Aaron and Miriam grumble against his leadership.

READ:
Numbers 11–12

Today's Date: _____   DAY 51

MY PRAYER FOR TODAY: ....
....
....

MY TAKEAWAY FROM TODAY'S READING:

....
....
....
....
....
....

Know Your Bible:

Moses sends twelve spies to observe the promised land. Ten frighten the people with reports of giants; God says only faithful Joshua and Caleb will enter Canaan.

READ:
Numbers 13–14

Today's Date: _____   DAY 52

MY PRAYER FOR TODAY: ....
....
....

Know Your Bible:

Doomed to forty years of wandering, the people are still instructed in how to worship the Lord. The rebellion of Korah the Levite leads to thousands of deaths.

READ:
Numbers 15–16

MY TAKEAWAY FROM TODAY'S READING:

....
....
....
....
....
....

DAY 53

Today's Date: _____

MY PRAYER FOR TODAY: ....
....
....

Know Your Bible:

Aaron's staff miraculously blossoms and produces almonds, proving that his family is God's chosen priesthood.

READ:
Numbers 17–19

MY TAKEAWAY FROM TODAY'S READING:

....
....
....
....
....
....

DAY 54

Today's Date: _____

MY PRAYER FOR TODAY: ....
....
....

MY TAKEAWAY FROM TODAY'S READING:

....
....
....
....
....
....

Know Your Bible:

An angry Moses disobeys God and is barred from the promised land. The complaining Israelites, plagued by venomous snakes, are healed by looking to a brass serpent on a pole.

READ:
Numbers 20–21

Today's Date: _____

DAY 55

MY PRAYER FOR TODAY: ....

....

....

MY TAKEAWAY FROM
TODAY'S READING:

....

....

....

....

....

....

*Know
Your Bible:*

An enemy king hires a pagan
prophet, Balaam, to curse the
Israelites; God causes Balaam
to bless them instead.

READ:
Numbers 22–24

Today's Date: _____

DAY 56

MY PRAYER FOR TODAY: ....

....

....

*Know
Your Bible:*

God requires another census
of Israel, numbering the new
generation that will enter
Canaan after the previous
generation has died off.
Joshua is appointed Moses'
successor.

READ:
Numbers 25–27

MY TAKEAWAY FROM
TODAY'S READING:

....

....

....

....

....

....

DAY 57

Today's Date: _____

MY PRAYER FOR TODAY: ....
....
....

Know Your Bible:

God tells Moses to remind the people of the various offerings and feasts to be observed once in Canaan.

READ:
Numbers 28–30

MY TAKEAWAY FROM TODAY'S READING:

....
....
....
....
....
....

DAY 58

Today's Date: _____

MY PRAYER FOR TODAY: ....
....
....

MY TAKEAWAY FROM TODAY'S READING:

....
....
....
....
....
....

Know Your Bible:

At God's command, Israel goes to war against Midian, which had earlier seduced the people with sexual sin and idolatry.

READ:
Numbers 31–32

Today's Date: _____

MY PRAYER FOR TODAY: ....
....
....

MY TAKEAWAY FROM
TODAY'S READING:

....
....
....
....
....
....

Know
Your Bible:

The Israelites prepare to enter
the promised land, with the
leader of each tribe desig-
nated to divide Canaan among
the people.

READ:
Numbers 33–34

Today's Date: _____

MY PRAYER FOR TODAY: ....
....
....

Know
Your Bible:

Israel's worship leaders, the
Levites, do not get their own
territory but will disperse
throughout Canaan in forty-
eight "cities of refuge."

READ:
Numbers 35–36

MY TAKEAWAY FROM
TODAY'S READING:

....
....
....
....
....
....

Today's Date: _____

MY PRAYER FOR TODAY: ....
....
....

Know Your Bible:

Moses reminds the Israelites of God's promise of land, the people's refusal to enter the land, and their forty-year punishment of wandering in the wilderness.

READ:
Deuteronomy 1–2

MY TAKEAWAY FROM TODAY'S READING:
....
....
....
....
....
....

Today's Date: _____

MY PRAYER FOR TODAY: ....
....
....

MY TAKEAWAY FROM TODAY'S READING:
....
....
....
....
....
....

Know Your Bible:

As the new generation of Israelites readies itself to enter Canaan, Moses teaches the people the "statutes and judgments" of God.

READ:
Deuteronomy 3–4

Today's Date: _____

MY PRAYER FOR TODAY: ....
....
....

MY TAKEAWAY FROM
TODAY'S READING:

....
....
....
....
....
....

*Know
Your Bible:*

Moses restates the Ten Commandments and shares the great rule, "Thou shalt love the LORD thy God with all thine heart, and with all thy soul, and with all thy might."

READ:
Deuteronomy 5–7

Today's Date: _____

MY PRAYER FOR TODAY: ....
....
....

*Know
Your Bible:*

Moses urges the people to honor God by remembering His care and provision for them during their decades in the wilderness.

READ:
Deuteronomy 8–11

MY TAKEAWAY FROM
TODAY'S READING:

....
....
....
....
....
....

DAY 65

Today's Date: _____

MY PRAYER FOR TODAY: ....
....
....

Know Your Bible:

Moses urges the Israelites to worship as God has commanded, and to destroy any vestiges of false worship and idolatry in Canaan.

READ:
Deuteronomy 12–14

MY TAKEAWAY FROM TODAY'S READING:

....
....
....
....
....
....

DAY 66

Today's Date: _____

MY PRAYER FOR TODAY: ....
....
....

MY TAKEAWAY FROM TODAY'S READING:

....
....
....
....
....

Know Your Bible:

Moses reminds the people to observe the Passover and other feasts, and predicts a day when the Israelites will demand a king to rule over them.

READ:
Deuteronomy 15–17

MY PRAYER FOR TODAY: ....
....
....

MY TAKEAWAY FROM
TODAY'S READING:

....
....
....
....
....
....

Know Your Bible:

Moses tells the people that God will one day raise up a prophet like himself—a hint at the life and ministry of Jesus.

READ:
Deuteronomy 18–20

MY PRAYER FOR TODAY: ....
....
....

Know Your Bible:

Moses proclaims various laws for Israel, including some that distinguish it from other nations—such as avoiding clothing of "divers sorts, as of woollen and linen together."

READ:
Deuteronomy 21–23

MY TAKEAWAY FROM
TODAY'S READING:

....
....
....
....
....
....

Today's Date: _____

MY PRAYER FOR TODAY: ....
....
....

Know Your Bible:

Moses explains additional laws for the people, including the law of firstfruits—they must offer God the first produce of the land.

READ:
Deuteronomy 24–26

MY TAKEAWAY FROM TODAY'S READING:

....
....
....
....
....
....

Today's Date: _____

MY PRAYER FOR TODAY: ....
....
....

MY TAKEAWAY FROM TODAY'S READING:

....
....
....
....
....
....

Know Your Bible:

Moses proclaims curses that will come on Israel for disobeying God, but blessings for following His commands.

READ:
Deuteronomy 27–28

Today's Date: _____

MY PRAYER FOR TODAY: ....
....
....

MY TAKEAWAY FROM
TODAY'S READING:

....

....

....

....

....

....

*Know
Your Bible:*

At age 120, Moses announces his impending death and charges Joshua to "bring the children of Israel into the land."

READ:
Deuteronomy 29–31

Today's Date: _____

MY PRAYER FOR TODAY: ....
....
....

*Know
Your Bible:*

Moses pronounces a final blessing over the people, then climbs Mount Pisgah for a glimpse of the promised land before he dies. Joshua assumes leadership of Israel.

READ:
Deuteronomy 32–34

MY TAKEAWAY FROM
TODAY'S READING:

....

....

....

....

....

....

Today's Date: _____

MY PRAYER FOR TODAY: ....
....
....

Know Your Bible:

God encourages Joshua in his new role as leader of Israel; he sends men to spy out the promised land at the fortified city of Jericho.

READ:
Joshua 1–2

MY TAKEAWAY FROM TODAY'S READING:

....
....
....
....
....
....

Today's Date: _____

MY PRAYER FOR TODAY: ....
....
....

MY TAKEAWAY FROM TODAY'S READING:

....
....
....
....
....
....

Know Your Bible:

To enter their promised land, the Israelites cross the Jordan River, miraculously parted by God. Joshua meets "the captain of the LORD's host."

READ:
Joshua 3–5

Today's Date: _____

MY PRAYER FOR TODAY: ....
....
....

MY TAKEAWAY FROM
TODAY'S READING:

....
....
....
....
....
....

*Know
Your Bible:*

Following God's battle plan—
march around Jericho and
watch its walls collapse—
Joshua and the Israelites begin their conquest of Canaan.

READ:
Joshua 6–8

Today's Date: _____

MY PRAYER FOR TODAY: ....
....
....

*Know
Your Bible:*

The people of Gibeon trick
the Israelites into letting them
live; Joshua honors the promise but makes the Gibeonites
servants to Israel.

READ:
Joshua 9–10

MY TAKEAWAY FROM
TODAY'S READING:

....
....
....
....
....
....

Today's Date: _____

MY PRAYER FOR TODAY: ....
....
....

Know Your Bible:

Joshua and the Israelite army defeat thirty-one pagan kings in their conquest of Canaan. The aging Joshua oversees distribution of the land to the individual tribes.

READ:
Joshua 11–13

MY TAKEAWAY FROM TODAY'S READING:

....
....
....
....
....
....

Today's Date: _____

MY PRAYER FOR TODAY: ....
....
....

MY TAKEAWAY FROM TODAY'S READING:

....
....
....
....
....
....

Know Your Bible:

Eighty-five-year-old Caleb, along with Joshua the only faithful spy sent to the promised land decades earlier, is given land as a reward.

READ:
Joshua 14–16

Today's Date: _____

MY PRAYER FOR TODAY: ....
....
....

MY TAKEAWAY FROM
TODAY'S READING:

....
....
....
....
....
....

*Know
Your Bible:*

With the promised land largely
in their hands, the Israelites
set up the tabernacle, their
tent of worship, at Shiloh.

READ:
Joshua 17–19

Today's Date: _____

MY PRAYER FOR TODAY: ....
....
....

*Know
Your Bible:*

Levites' cities of refuge are
established, while tribes set-
tling east of the Jordan (Reu-
ben, Gad, half of Manasseh)
defend the erection of an
altar to God in their territory.

READ:
Joshua 20–22

MY TAKEAWAY FROM
TODAY'S READING:

....
....
....
....
....
....

Today's Date: _____

MY PRAYER FOR TODAY: ....
....
....

Know Your Bible:

The dying Joshua issues a final charge to Israel: "Choose you this day whom ye will serve. . . as for me and my house, we will serve the LORD."

READ:
Joshua 23–24

MY TAKEAWAY FROM TODAY'S READING:

....
....
....
....
....
....

Today's Date: _____

MY PRAYER FOR TODAY: ....
....
....

MY TAKEAWAY FROM TODAY'S READING:

....
....
....
....
....
....

Know Your Bible:

Israel fails to drive out every inhabitant of Canaan, and the pagan people become "thorns in [their] sides." God raises up leaders called judges to defeat Israel's enemies.

READ:
Judges 1–3

Today's Date: _____

MY PRAYER FOR TODAY: ....

....

....

MY TAKEAWAY FROM
TODAY'S READING:

....

....

....

....

....

....

*Know
Your Bible:*

Israel's only female judge,
the prophet Deborah, leads
the army to victory over the
enemy general Sisera.

READ:
Judges 4–5

Today's Date: _____

MY PRAYER FOR TODAY: ....

....

....

*Know
Your Bible:*

God calls the insecure Gideon
to be a judge; with only three
hundred men, he miraculously
destroys the "host of Midian."

READ:
Judges 6–8

MY TAKEAWAY FROM
TODAY'S READING:

....

....

....

....

....

....

Today's Date: _____

MY PRAYER FOR TODAY: ....
....
....

Know Your Bible:

After Gideon's death, one of his seventy sons (born to a concubine) aspires to leadership. But he is wicked and dies when a woman in a tower drops a millstone on his head.

READ:
Judges 9

MY TAKEAWAY FROM TODAY'S READING:
....
....
....
....
....
....

Today's Date: _____

MY PRAYER FOR TODAY: ....
....
....

MY TAKEAWAY FROM TODAY'S READING:
....
....
....
....
....
....

Know Your Bible:

The exploits of several judges are recorded, including those of Jephthah, who lost his daughter after making a rash and foolish vow to God.

READ:
Judges 10–12

Today's Date: _____

MY PRAYER FOR TODAY: ....
....
....

MY TAKEAWAY FROM TODAY'S READING:

....
....
....
....
....
....

Know Your Bible:

The miraculously strong Samson judges Israel, but he is derailed by selfish appetites. He will die along with thousands of enemy Philistines when he collapses their temple.

READ:
Judges 13–16

Today's Date: _____

MY PRAYER FOR TODAY: ....
....
....

Know Your Bible:

After Samson's death, leaderless Israel devolves into idolatry and conflict between tribes.

READ:
Judges 17–19

MY TAKEAWAY FROM TODAY'S READING:

....
....
....
....
....
....

Today's Date: _____

MY PRAYER FOR TODAY: ....
....
....

Know Your Bible:

Conflict in Israel breaks out into civil war. Sadly, in the days without a king, "every man did that which was right in his own eyes."

READ:
Judges 20–21

MY TAKEAWAY FROM TODAY'S READING:

....
....
....
....
....
....

Today's Date: _____

MY PRAYER FOR TODAY: ....
....
....

MY TAKEAWAY FROM TODAY'S READING:

....
....
....
....
....
....

Know Your Bible:

A pagan Moabite, widow of an Israelite, commits to her mother-in-law and God. Ruth will become great-grandmother of King David.

READ:
Ruth 1–4

MY PRAYER FOR TODAY: ....
....
....

MY TAKEAWAY FROM
TODAY'S READING:

....
....
....
....
....
....

*Know
Your Bible:*

Hannah, an infertile woman, prays for a son and God answers with Samuel, who will become the prophet and priest of Israel.

READ:
1 Samuel 1–3

MY PRAYER FOR TODAY: ....
....
....

*Know
Your Bible:*

Israel's priest, Eli, dies upon learning that his two sons had died in battle against the Philistines.

READ:
1 Samuel 4–6

MY TAKEAWAY FROM
TODAY'S READING:

....
....
....
....
....
....

DAY 93

MY PRAYER FOR TODAY: ....
....
....

Know Your Bible:

Samuel prays Israel to victory over the Philistines; years later, his corrupt sons cause people to demand a king. God instructs Samuel to choose Saul.

READ:
1 Samuel 7–9

MY TAKEAWAY FROM TODAY'S READING:

....
....
....
....
....
....

DAY 94

Today's Date: _____

MY PRAYER FOR TODAY: ....
....
....

MY TAKEAWAY FROM TODAY'S READING:

....
....
....
....
....
....

Know Your Bible:

Saul is anointed as king, and he begins with an impressive military victory over the Ammonites.

READ:
1 Samuel 10–12

Today's Date: _____

MY PRAYER FOR TODAY: ....
....
....

MY TAKEAWAY FROM
TODAY'S READING:

....
....
....
....
....
....

Know Your Bible:

Saul foolishly intrudes on the duties of the priests, making a burnt offering while waiting for Samuel. Samuel says God will replace Saul with "a man after his own heart."

READ:
1 Samuel 13–14

Today's Date: _____

MY PRAYER FOR TODAY: ....
....
....

Know Your Bible:

Saul disobeys God's command to completely destroy the Amalekites, and God directs Samuel to a shepherd boy named David to be Saul's successor.

READ:
1 Samuel 15–16

MY TAKEAWAY FROM
TODAY'S READING:

....
....
....
....
....

DAY 97

Today's Date: _____

MY PRAYER FOR TODAY: ....
....
....

Know Your Bible:

David gains the love of the nation of Israel—and the envy of Saul—by defeating the Philistine giant Goliath with a slung stone.

READ:
1 Samuel 17–18

MY TAKEAWAY FROM TODAY'S READING:

....
....
....
....
....
....
....

DAY 98

Today's Date: _____

MY PRAYER FOR TODAY: ....
....
....

MY TAKEAWAY FROM TODAY'S READING:

....
....
....
....
....
....

Know Your Bible:

Saul tries numerous times to kill David, who is protected by God and by Saul's son Jonathan, heir to the throne but best friend of David.

READ:
1 Samuel 19–20

Today's Date: _____

MY PRAYER FOR TODAY: ....

....

....

MY TAKEAWAY FROM TODAY'S READING:

....

....

....

....

....

....

Know Your Bible:

David runs from Saul, gathers a group of some four hundred fighting men, and hides in the wilderness.

READ:
1 Samuel 21–23

Today's Date: _____

MY PRAYER FOR TODAY: ....

....

....

Know Your Bible:

Given an opportunity to kill Saul, David declines, calling him "the LORD's anointed." Samuel dies. David marries Abigail, widow of the foolish Nabal.

READ:
1 Samuel 24–25

MY TAKEAWAY FROM TODAY'S READING:

....

....

....

....

....

....

Today's Date: _____

MY PRAYER FOR TODAY: ....
....
....

Know Your Bible:

David again spares Saul's life, then seeks shelter among the enemy Philistines. Saul seeks the dead Samuel's guidance through a forbidden medium, and learns he will soon die.

READ:
1 Samuel 26–28

MY TAKEAWAY FROM TODAY'S READING:
....
....
....
....
....
....

Today's Date: _____

MY PRAYER FOR TODAY: ....
....
....

MY TAKEAWAY FROM TODAY'S READING:
....
....
....
....
....
....

Know Your Bible:

David has ingratiated himself with an enemy commander. Caught in his deceit when Philistines prepare to fight Israel, he is expelled and not present when Saul is killed.

READ:
1 Samuel 29–31

Today's Date: _____ **DAY 103**

MY PRAYER FOR TODAY: ....
....
....

MY TAKEAWAY FROM
TODAY'S READING:

....
....
....
....
....
....

*Know
Your Bible:*

David learns of Saul's death,
mourns for him and Jona-
than, and is made king over
the southern region of Israel
called Judah.

READ:
2 Samuel 1–2

Today's Date: _____ **DAY 104**

MY PRAYER FOR TODAY: ....
....
....

*Know
Your Bible:*

David rules from Hebron,
fighting with Saul's son Ish-
bosheth, king of Israel's northern region. In seven years,
Ish-bosheth is murdered by
two of his military captains.

READ:
2 Samuel 3–4

MY TAKEAWAY FROM
TODAY'S READING:

....
....
....
....
....
....

DAY 105

Today's Date: _____

MY PRAYER FOR TODAY: ....
....
....

Know Your Bible:

David becomes king over all Israel, brings the ark of the covenant to Jerusalem, and hopes to build a temple. God says no but promises an on-going dynasty for David.

READ:
2 Samuel 5–7

MY TAKEAWAY FROM TODAY'S READING:

....
....
....
....
....
....

DAY 106

Today's Date: _____

MY PRAYER FOR TODAY: ....
....
....

MY TAKEAWAY FROM TODAY'S READING:

....
....
....
....
....
....

Know Your Bible:

David subdues many of Israel's enemies through military victories, and generously welcomes Saul's disabled grandson, Mephibosheth, to live in his palace.

READ:
2 Samuel 8–10

Today's Date: _____

MY PRAYER FOR TODAY: ....
....
....

MY TAKEAWAY FROM TODAY'S READING:

....
....
....
....
....
....

Know Your Bible:

David sleeps with his neighbor's wife, then has the man killed. He repents, but God says "the sword shall never depart" from his home. Solomon is born to the woman, now David's wife.

READ:
2 Samuel 11–12

Today's Date: _____

MY PRAYER FOR TODAY: ....
....
....

Know Your Bible:

David's family crumbles, as one son violates a half sister, only to be killed by the girl's full brother, David's handsome and ambitious son Absalom.

READ:
2 Samuel 13–14

MY TAKEAWAY FROM TODAY'S READING:

....
....
....
....
....
....

Today's Date: _____

MY PRAYER FOR TODAY: ....
....
....

Know
Your Bible:

Absalom conspires to usurp
the kingship from his father,
forcing David to flee from
Jerusalem.

READ:
2 Samuel 15–16

MY TAKEAWAY FROM
TODAY'S READING:

....
....
....
....
....
....

Today's Date: _____

MY PRAYER FOR TODAY: ....
....
....

MY TAKEAWAY FROM
TODAY'S READING:

....
....
....
....
....
....

Know
Your Bible:

Soldiers in support of both
David and Absalom battle
in the woods of Ephraim,
where Absalom is killed. David
mourns deeply for his lost son.

READ:
2 Samuel 17–18

Today's Date: _____ DAY III

MY PRAYER FOR TODAY: ....
....
....

MY TAKEAWAY FROM
TODAY'S READING:

....
....
....
....
....
....

*Know
Your Bible:*

Israel is divided, with squabbling among supporters of David and the deceased Absalom as the king returns to Jerusalem.

READ:
2 Samuel 19–20

Today's Date: _____ DAY II2

MY PRAYER FOR TODAY: ....
....
....

*Know
Your Bible:*

David must once again fight the Philistines, including descendants of the giant Goliath. He writes a psalm of praise to God for deliverance.

READ:
2 Samuel 21–22

MY TAKEAWAY FROM
TODAY'S READING:

....
....
....
....
....
....

Today's Date: _____

MY PRAYER FOR TODAY: ....
....
....

Know Your Bible:

David counts his fighting men, apparently trusting his military strength over God's power, and suffers the loss of seventy thousand men as punishment.

READ:
2 Samuel 23–24

MY TAKEAWAY FROM TODAY'S READING:
....
....
....
....
....
....

Today's Date: _____

MY PRAYER FOR TODAY: ....
....
....

MY TAKEAWAY FROM TODAY'S READING:
....
....
....
....
....
....

Know Your Bible:

The ailing David announces that Solomon will succeed him as king, bypassing an older son. Upon David's death, Solomon consolidates power by executing several enemies.

READ:
1 Kings 1–2

Today's Date: _____

MY PRAYER FOR TODAY:

....
....
....

MY TAKEAWAY FROM TODAY'S READING:

....
....
....
....
....
....

Know Your Bible:

God offers Solomon anything he wants, and the new king requests wisdom. Pleased with this response, God also promises Solomon wealth and fame.

READ:
1 Kings 3–4

Today's Date: _____

MY PRAYER FOR TODAY:

....
....
....

Know Your Bible:

Solomon erects the temple for God that his father, David, had hoped to build. The construction takes seven years; Solomon spends thirteen years building his own palace.

READ:
1 Kings 5–7

MY TAKEAWAY FROM TODAY'S READING:

....
....
....
....
....
....

Today's Date: _____

MY PRAYER FOR TODAY: ....
....
....

Know Your Bible:

Solomon brings the ark of the covenant to its permanent home in the Jerusalem temple. God warns that idolatry in Israel will lead to the hallowed building's ruin.

READ:
1 Kings 8–9

MY TAKEAWAY FROM TODAY'S READING:

....
....
....
....
....
....

Today's Date: _____

MY PRAYER FOR TODAY: ....
....
....

MY TAKEAWAY FROM TODAY'S READING:

....
....
....
....
....
....

Know Your Bible:

Fabulously wealthy, Solomon marries seven hundred women, who turn his heart toward idols. God raises up a rival, one of Solomon's officials named Jeroboam.

READ:
1 Kings 10–11

Today's Date: _____

MY PRAYER FOR TODAY: ·······················
···
···

MY TAKEAWAY FROM
TODAY'S READING:

·······································
·······································
·······································
·······································
·······································
·······································

Know Your Bible:

After Solomon dies, his son Rehoboam becomes king and foolishly antagonizes the people. Ten northern tribes break away and make Jeroboam their king.

READ:
1 Kings 12–13

Today's Date: _____

MY PRAYER FOR TODAY: ·······················
···
···

Know Your Bible:

Israel suffers from a succession of evil kings. In Judah, Rehoboam and his son Abijam are wicked, but Abijam's son Asa follows God.

READ:
1 Kings 14–15

MY TAKEAWAY FROM
TODAY'S READING:

·······································
·······································
·······································
·······································
·······································
·······································

DAY 121

Today's Date: _____

MY PRAYER FOR TODAY: ....
....
....

Know Your Bible:

Israel's poor leadership continues under several kings, with the worst of all being Ahab. The prophet Elijah predicts a drought and raises a widow's son from the dead.

READ:
1 Kings 16–17

MY TAKEAWAY FROM TODAY'S READING:

....
....
....
....
....
....

DAY 122

Today's Date: _____

MY PRAYER FOR TODAY: ....
....
....

MY TAKEAWAY FROM TODAY'S READING:

....
....
....
....
....

Know Your Bible:

Elijah confronts Ahab and his queen, Jezebel, for their Baal worship, and defeats hundreds of false prophets on Mount Carmel. Then he calls Elisha to be his successor.

READ:
1 Kings 18–19

Today's Date: _____

MY PRAYER FOR TODAY: ....
....
....

MY TAKEAWAY FROM
TODAY'S READING:

....
....
....
....
....
....

*Know
Your Bible:*

Ahab covets a neighbor's vineyard, and Jezebel frames the man with a false charge of blasphemy, a capital offense. Elijah pronounces doom on Ahab and his family line.

READ:
1 Kings 20–21

Today's Date: _____

MY PRAYER FOR TODAY: ....
....
....

*Know
Your Bible:*

King Ahab of Israel dies in battle and is replaced by his evil son Ahaziah; in Judah, Asa's son Jehoshaphat begins a positive twenty-five-year reign.

READ:
1 Kings 22

MY TAKEAWAY FROM
TODAY'S READING:

....
....
....
....
....
....

Today's Date: _____

MY PRAYER FOR TODAY: ....
....
....

Know Your Bible:

Elijah is taken directly to heaven in a chariot of fire and Elisha becomes the main prophet in Israel.

READ:
2 Kings 1–3

MY TAKEAWAY FROM TODAY'S READING:

....
....
....
....
....
....

Today's Date: _____

MY PRAYER FOR TODAY: ....
....
....

MY TAKEAWAY FROM TODAY'S READING:

....
....
....
....
....
....

Know Your Bible:

Elisha performs many miracles: increasing a widow's oil supply, raising another woman's son from the dead, and curing a Syrian commander's leprosy.

READ:
2 Kings 4–5

Today's Date: _____

MY PRAYER FOR TODAY: ·····································
··
··

MY TAKEAWAY FROM
TODAY'S READING:

···································
···································
···································
···································
···································
···································

Know Your Bible:

Elisha predicts the breaking of a Syrian siege of Samaria and a seven-year famine in Israel. Judah's kings, Jehoram and Ahaziah, are wicked.

READ:
2 Kings 6–8

Today's Date: _____

DAY 128

MY PRAYER FOR TODAY: ·····································
··
··

Know Your Bible:

Elisha appoints Jehu king of Israel; he fulfills God's prophecy by killing Ahab's wife, Jezebel, and their son, King Joram. Jehu then destroys Baal worship in Israel.

READ:
2 Kings 9–10

MY TAKEAWAY FROM
TODAY'S READING:

···································
···································
···································
···································
···································
···································

Today's Date: _____

MY PRAYER FOR TODAY: ....
....
....

Know Your Bible:

A royal seven-year-old in Judah, Joash, is protected from intrigue and violence and becomes king. His early reign sees revival and the repair of God's temple in Jerusalem.

READ:
2 Kings 11–13

MY TAKEAWAY FROM TODAY'S READING:

....
....
....
....
....

Today's Date: _____

MY PRAYER FOR TODAY: ....
....
....

MY TAKEAWAY FROM TODAY'S READING:

....
....
....
....
....

Know Your Bible:

Numerous kings, all of them bad, rule over Israel; Judah's kings are a mixed lot, with Azariah (also known as Uzziah) and his son Jotham being generally good.

READ:
2 Kings 14–15

Today's Date: _____ 　　　**DAY 131**

MY PRAYER FOR TODAY: ....
....
....

MY TAKEAWAY FROM
TODAY'S READING:

....
....
....
....
....
....

*Know
Your Bible:*

Israel's sin finally brings
judgment in the form of an
Assyrian invasion. The people
of Israel are forced to leave
their country, while outsiders
are settled in their place.

READ:
2 Kings 16–17

Today's Date: _____ 　　　**DAY 132**

MY PRAYER FOR TODAY: ....
....
....

*Know
Your Bible:*

Judah's godly King Hezekiah
faces an invasion by a huge
Assyrian army; the king's
humble prayer leads to God's
destruction of 185,000
enemy soldiers.

READ:
2 Kings 18–19

MY TAKEAWAY FROM
TODAY'S READING:

....
....
....
....
....
....

DAY 133

Today's Date: _____

MY PRAYER FOR TODAY: ....
....
....

Know Your Bible:

Afflicted with a terminal disease, Hezekiah prays. The prophet Isaiah says God will give him an additional fifteen years of life. He is succeeded by an evil son, Manasseh.

READ:
2 Kings 20–21

MY TAKEAWAY FROM TODAY'S READING:

....
....
....
....
....
....

DAY 134

Today's Date: _____

MY PRAYER FOR TODAY: ....
....
....

MY TAKEAWAY FROM TODAY'S READING:

....
....
....
....
....
....

Know Your Bible:

Another young king, eight-year-old Josiah, leads Judah into respect for God and His laws. After a thirty-one-year reign, he dies in battle with Egypt.

READ:
2 Kings 22:1–23:30

Today's Date: _____

MY PRAYER FOR TODAY: ....

....

....

MY TAKEAWAY FROM TODAY'S READING:

....

....

....

....

....

....

Know Your Bible:

Judah's final four kings are wicked, and the nation is invaded by the Babylonians under King Nebuchadnezzar. Jerusalem is plundered and many people deported.

READ:
2 Kings 23:31–25:30

Today's Date: _____

MY PRAYER FOR TODAY: ....

....

....

Know Your Bible:

Covering many of the events of the books of Samuel and Kings, 1 Chronicles emphasizes the nation of Judah, beginning with a genealogy of Jacob's son Judah to King David.

READ:
1 Chronicles 1–4

MY TAKEAWAY FROM TODAY'S READING:

....

....

....

....

....

....

Today's Date: _____

MY PRAYER FOR TODAY: ·····················
··
··

Know Your Bible:

Briefer genealogies of the other sons of Jacob are provided, with an emphasis on the priestly line of Levi.

READ:
1 Chronicles 5–7

MY TAKEAWAY FROM TODAY'S READING:

·····················
·····················
·····················
·····················
·····················
·····················

Today's Date: _____

MY PRAYER FOR TODAY: ·····················
··
··

MY TAKEAWAY FROM TODAY'S READING:

·····················
·····················
·····················
·····················
·····················
·····················

Know Your Bible:

The tribe of Benjamin, family line of Israel's first king (Saul), is highlighted, capped by an account of Saul's death in battle against the Philistines.

READ:
1 Chronicles 8–10

Today's Date: _____   DAY 139

MY PRAYER FOR TODAY: ....

....

....

MY TAKEAWAY FROM
TODAY'S READING:

....

....

....

....

....

....

*Know
Your Bible*:

David's accession to the throne is described, along with listings of his key soldiers and his wives and children.

READ:
1 Chronicles 11–14

Today's Date: _____   DAY 140

MY PRAYER FOR TODAY: ....

....

....

*Know
Your Bible*:

David moves the ark of the covenant into his capital of Jerusalem, with great celebration and sacrifice. God promises David a "kingdom for ever."

READ:
1 Chronicles 15–17

MY TAKEAWAY FROM
TODAY'S READING:

....

....

....

....

....

....

DAY 141

Today's Date: _____

MY PRAYER FOR TODAY: ....
....
....

Know Your Bible:

David's kingdom is established by his military successes, but he sins when he decides to count his fighting men. God punishes Israel with a three-day plague.

READ:
1 Chronicles 18–21

MY TAKEAWAY FROM TODAY'S READING:

....
....
....
....
....
....

DAY 142

Today's Date: _____

MY PRAYER FOR TODAY: ....
....
....

MY TAKEAWAY FROM TODAY'S READING:

....
....
....
....
....
....

Know Your Bible:

David prepares material for God's temple, which his son Solomon will build. David names Solomon his successor as king.

READ:
1 Chronicles 22–24

Today's Date: _____ **DAY 143**

....
....
....

MY TAKEAWAY FROM TODAY'S READING:

....
....
....
....
....
....

Know Your Bible:

David organizes worship leaders, temple overseers, and other officers for the nation of Israel.

READ:
1 Chronicles 25–27

Today's Date: _____ **DAY 144**

MY PRAYER FOR TODAY: ....
....
....

Know Your Bible:

David publicly announces Solomon as Israel's next king, encouraging the people to support Solomon in building God's temple. David dies after forty years as king.

READ:
1 Chronicles 28–29

MY TAKEAWAY FROM TODAY'S READING:

....
....
....
....
....
....

Today's Date: _____

MY PRAYER FOR TODAY: ....
....
....

Know Your Bible:

In a vision, God offers Solomon anything he wishes; the new king chooses wisdom. In the fourth year of his reign, Solomon begins building God's temple.

READ:
2 Chronicles 1–4

MY TAKEAWAY FROM TODAY'S READING:

....
....
....
....
....
....

Today's Date: _____

MY PRAYER FOR TODAY: ....
....
....

MY TAKEAWAY FROM TODAY'S READING:

....
....
....
....
....
....

Know Your Bible:

The temple complete, Solomon installs the ark of the covenant, prays publicly, and receives God's promise of blessing for obedience and punishment for disobedience.

READ:
2 Chronicles 5–7

Today's Date: _____

MY PRAYER FOR TODAY: ....
....
....

MY TAKEAWAY FROM TODAY'S READING:

....
....
....
....
....
....

Know Your Bible:

As God had promised Solomon, he would be wise, famous, and wealthy. The visiting queen of Sheba marvels at his bounty. After a forty-year reign, Solomon dies.

READ:
2 Chronicles 8–9

Today's Date: _____

MY PRAYER FOR TODAY: ....
....
....

Know Your Bible:

Solomon's son Rehoboam becomes king and foolishly antagonizes the people; ten northern tribes rebel and name their own king, Jeroboam.

READ:
2 Chronicles 10–13

MY TAKEAWAY FROM TODAY'S READING:

....
....
....
....
....
....

Today's Date: _____

MY PRAYER FOR TODAY: ....
....
....

Know Your Bible:

Separate Jewish kingdoms, Israel and Judah, go through years of conflict under a succession of generally flawed kings.

READ:
2 Chronicles 14–18

MY TAKEAWAY FROM TODAY'S READING:

....
....
....
....
....
....

Today's Date: _____

MY PRAYER FOR TODAY: ....
....
....

MY TAKEAWAY FROM TODAY'S READING:

....
....
....
....
....
....

Know Your Bible:

Judah's King Jehoshaphat rules well, restoring order in worship and successfully resisting an invasion. But he is succeeded by a wicked son, Jehoram.

READ:
2 Chronicles 19–21

Today's Date: _____

MY PRAYER FOR TODAY: ·······································
··
··

MY TAKEAWAY FROM
TODAY'S READING:

··
··
··
··
··
··

Know Your Bible:

Jehoram's son Ahaziah rules wickedly and dies in battle. A seven-year-old son, Joash, is made king; his forty-year reign starts well, but he orders a prophet's death and is assassinated.

READ:
2 Chronicles 22–24

Today's Date: _____

MY PRAYER FOR TODAY: ·································
··
··

Know Your Bible:

Judah is wracked by war, even with the northern kingdom of Israel. Uzziah (also called Azariah) rules well but contracts leprosy after pridefully intruding into the temple.

READ:
2 Chronicles 25–28

MY TAKEAWAY FROM
TODAY'S READING:

··
··
··
··
··
··

Today's Date: _____

MY PRAYER FOR TODAY: ....
....
....

Know Your Bible:

A very good king, Hezekiah, rules Judah, overseeing a spiritual revival, restoration of temple worship, and the keeping of the Passover.

READ:
2 Chronicles 29–30

MY TAKEAWAY FROM TODAY'S READING:

....
....
....
....
....
....

Today's Date: _____

MY PRAYER FOR TODAY: ....
....
....

MY TAKEAWAY FROM TODAY'S READING:

....
....
....
....
....
....

Know Your Bible:

Hezekiah destroys idols in Judah and prayerfully resists an Assyrian invasion. His son Manasseh succeeds him on the throne, but does "evil in the sight of the LORD."

READ:
2 Chronicles 31–33

Today's Date: _____ ➤ DAY 155

MY PRAYER FOR TODAY: ....
....
....

MY TAKEAWAY FROM
TODAY'S READING:

....
....
....
....
....
....

*Know
Your Bible:*

Judah's history winds down
with one good king (Josiah)
and several wicked ones, before the nation is invaded and
its people deported by the
Babylonians.

READ:
2 Chronicles 34–36

Today's Date: _____ ➤ DAY 156

MY PRAYER FOR TODAY: ....
....
....

*Know
Your Bible:*

Cyrus, king of Persia (con-
queror of Babylon) allows exiled Jews to return to Judah.
Some forty-two thousand go,
and begin laying a foundation
for the ruined temple.

READ:
Ezra 1–3

MY TAKEAWAY FROM
TODAY'S READING:

....
....
....
....
....
....

DAY 157

Today's Date: _____

MY PRAYER FOR TODAY: ....
....
....

Know Your Bible:

Enemies try to stop the Jews' rebuilding of the temple, but a new king, Darius, allows them to continue. The work is done some seventy years after the Babylonian destruction.

READ:
Ezra 4–6

MY TAKEAWAY FROM TODAY'S READING:

....
....
....
....
....
....

DAY 158

Today's Date: _____

MY PRAYER FOR TODAY: ....
....
....

MY TAKEAWAY FROM TODAY'S READING:

....
....
....
....
....
....

Know Your Bible:

Ezra, an exiled priest, travels to Jerusalem "to teach in Israel statutes and judgments."

READ:
Ezra 7–8

Today's Date: _____ → **DAY 159**

MY PRAYER FOR TODAY: ....
....
....

MY TAKEAWAY FROM TODAY'S READING:

....
....
....
....
....
....

Know Your Bible:

Ezra is disturbed to learn many Jews have broken God's law by marrying foreign women. He urges them to "put away" these wives, and many do.

READ:
Ezra 9–10

Today's Date: _____ → **DAY 160**

MY PRAYER FOR TODAY: ....
....
....

Know Your Bible:

The Jewish exile Nehemiah works for the Persian king Artaxerxes, and receives his approval to return to Jerusalem to rebuild its broken walls.

READ:
Nehemiah 1–3

MY TAKEAWAY FROM TODAY'S READING:

....
....
....
....
....

DAY 161

Today's Date: _____

MY PRAYER FOR TODAY: ....
....
....

Know Your Bible:

Enemies of the Jews employ several strategies to stop the rebuilding work, but the walls are done in fifty-two days. Nehemiah notes "this work was wrought of our God."

READ:
Nehemiah 4–6

MY TAKEAWAY FROM TODAY'S READING:

....
....
....
....
....
....

DAY 162

Today's Date: _____

MY PRAYER FOR TODAY: ....
....
....

MY TAKEAWAY FROM TODAY'S READING:

....
....
....
....
....
....

Know Your Bible:

Ezra reappears, reading and explaining God's law to the people. The Jews fast and repent of their sins.

READ:
Nehemiah 7–9

Today's Date: _____

MY PRAYER FOR TODAY: ··
···
···

MY TAKEAWAY FROM
TODAY'S READING:

·································
·································
·································
·································
·································
·································

*Know
Your Bible:*

The people promise to ob-
serve their covenant with
God, calling a curse on themselves if they fail.

READ:
Nehemiah 10–11

Today's Date: _____

MY PRAYER FOR TODAY: ····································
···
···

*Know
Your Bible:*

Nehemiah addresses several
failings of the people—for-
eigners in the temple, Levites
neglecting their duty, work
on the Sabbath. He prays,
"Remember me, O my God,
for good."

READ:
Nehemiah 12–13

MY TAKEAWAY FROM
TODAY'S READING:

·································
·································
·································
·································
·································
·································

Today's Date: _____

MY PRAYER FOR TODAY: ....

....

....

Know Your Bible:

In Persia, a beautiful Jewish exile named Esther becomes queen when the king chooses her from his harem. A royal advisor, Haman, plots against the Jews.

READ:
Esther 1–3

MY TAKEAWAY FROM TODAY'S READING:

....

....

....

....

....

....

Today's Date: _____

MY PRAYER FOR TODAY: ....

....

....

MY TAKEAWAY FROM TODAY'S READING:

....

....

....

....

....

....

Know Your Bible:

Approaching the king without an invitation can be punished by death, but Esther bravely enters his presence to plead for her people.

READ:
Esther 4–6

Today's Date: _____ DAY 167

MY PRAYER FOR TODAY: ....
....
....

MY TAKEAWAY FROM
TODAY'S READING:

....
....
....
....
....
....

*Know
Your Bible:*

Haman is executed and the
Jews are allowed to defend
themselves against his mur-
derous plot. The feast of
Purim is begun as a memorial.

READ:
Esther 7–10

Today's Date: _____ DAY 168

MY PRAYER FOR TODAY: ....
....
....

*Know
Your Bible:*

A good man named Job loses
his children, wealth, and
health in a short time, un-
aware that God has allowed
Satan's attacks to prove Job's
righteousness.

READ:
Job 1–5

MY TAKEAWAY FROM
TODAY'S READING:

....
....
....
....
....
....

DAY 169

Today's Date: _____

MY PRAYER FOR TODAY: ....
....
....

Know Your Bible:

Three friends accompany Job in his misery, but soon begin questioning why he is suffering so badly. Bildad accuses the righteous Job of hypocrisy.

READ:
Job 6–10

MY TAKEAWAY FROM TODAY'S READING:
....
....
....
....
....
....

DAY 170

Today's Date: _____

MY PRAYER FOR TODAY: ....
....
....

MY TAKEAWAY FROM TODAY'S READING:
....
....
....
....
....
....

Know Your Bible:

Job's friend Zophar accuses Job of lying. Job defends himself, but seems to be losing hope.

READ:
Job 11–14

Today's Date: _____　　　　　**DAY 171**

MY PRAYER FOR TODAY: ....
....
....

MY TAKEAWAY FROM
TODAY'S READING:

....
....
....
....
....
....

*Know
Your Bible:*

Eliphaz insinuates that Job has hidden sins. Job cries, "Miserable comforters are ye all." Though he feels God is persecuting him, Job says, "I know that my redeemer liveth."

READ:
Job 15–19

Today's Date: _____　　　　　**DAY 172**

MY PRAYER FOR TODAY: ....
....
....

*Know
Your Bible:*

Job longs to talk with God, to have an opportunity to present his case before Him.

READ:
Job 20–24

MY TAKEAWAY FROM
TODAY'S READING:

....
....
....
....
....
....

Today's Date: _____

MY PRAYER FOR TODAY: ....
....
....

Know Your Bible:

Job continues to defend himself, noting how he had made a covenant with his eyes not to "think upon a maid." He knows that God recognizes his innocence.

READ:
Job 25–31

MY TAKEAWAY FROM TODAY'S READING:

....
....
....
....
....
....

Today's Date: _____

MY PRAYER FOR TODAY: ....
....
....

MY TAKEAWAY FROM TODAY'S READING:

....
....
....
....
....

Know Your Bible:

Another man, Elihu, arrives to criticize all: Job, "because he justified himself rather than God" and the friends, "because they had found no answer, and yet had condemned Job."

READ:
Job 32–37

Today's Date: _____

MY PRAYER FOR TODAY: ....
....
....

MY TAKEAWAY FROM
TODAY'S READING:

....
....
....
....
....
....

Know Your Bible:

Job finally hears from God, who poses questions proving His superior wisdom. Job repents and prays for his friends. God restores Job's wealth and family.

READ:
Job 38–42

Today's Date: _____

MY PRAYER FOR TODAY: ....
....
....

Know Your Bible:

God "knoweth the way of the righteous," is a shield to the persecuted, and a refuge in times of trouble. Though He created the stars, He is mindful of humanity.

READ:
Psalms 1–10

MY TAKEAWAY FROM
TODAY'S READING:

....
....
....
....
....
....

DAY 177

MY PRAYER FOR TODAY: ....
....
....

Know Your Bible:

Fools believe there is no God; evil talkers are barred from His presence. The psalm writer extols the Lord's faithfulness to His promises to David and his family.

READ:
Psalms 11–18

MY TAKEAWAY FROM TODAY'S READING:

....
....
....
....
....
....

DAY 178

MY PRAYER FOR TODAY: ....
....
....

MY TAKEAWAY FROM TODAY'S READING:

....
....
....
....
....
....

Know Your Bible:

Creation declares God's glory. The Lord is a shepherd to His people. With God as "my light and my salvation," there is no need to fear.

READ:
Psalms 19–27

Today's Date: _____

MY PRAYER FOR TODAY: ....
....
....

MY TAKEAWAY FROM
TODAY'S READING:

....
....
....
....
....
....

Know Your Bible:

God's anger is brief, but "joy cometh in the morning." Confession of sin brings forgiveness and happiness. God is near to the brokenhearted and contrite.

READ:
Psalms 28–34

Today's Date: _____

MY PRAYER FOR TODAY: ....
....
....

Know Your Bible:

Evildoers are not to be envied, because they will soon fall; the meek will inherit the earth. God does not forsake His people.

READ:
Psalms 35–39

MY TAKEAWAY FROM
TODAY'S READING:

....
....
....
....
....
....

Today's Date: _____

MY PRAYER FOR TODAY: ....
....
....

Know Your Bible:

Wait patiently for God, and He will listen. The Lord honors those who help the poor. He is His people's refuge and strength, "a very present help in trouble."

READ:
Psalms 40–47

MY TAKEAWAY FROM TODAY'S READING:

....
....
....
....
....
....

Today's Date: _____

MY PRAYER FOR TODAY: ....
....
....

MY TAKEAWAY FROM TODAY'S READING:

....
....
....
....
....
....

Know Your Bible:

Call on God in the day of trouble, and He will deliver you. Humble, personal admission of sin—as of David with Bathsheba—God "wilt not despise."

READ:
Psalms 48–55

Today's Date: _____

MY PRAYER FOR TODAY: ....
....
....

MY TAKEAWAY FROM
TODAY'S READING:

....

....

....

....

....

....

*Know
Your Bible:*

Look to God for help in trouble, "for vain is the help of man." Power belongs to God.

READ:
Psalms 56–65

Today's Date: _____

MY PRAYER FOR TODAY: ....
....
....

*Know
Your Bible:*

Praise God in song for His powerful works. Don't treasure sin in your heart, or else "the LORD will not hear." God is our hope; we go on in His strength.

READ:
Psalms 66–71

MY TAKEAWAY FROM
TODAY'S READING:

....

....

....

....

....

....

Today's Date: _____

MY PRAYER FOR TODAY: ....
....
....

Know Your Bible:

The wicked may seem to succeed but face a terrible end. The Lord is to be feared: "who is so great a God as our God?"

READ:
Psalms 72–77

MY TAKEAWAY FROM TODAY'S READING:

....
....
....
....
....
....

Today's Date: _____

MY PRAYER FOR TODAY: ....
....
....

MY TAKEAWAY FROM TODAY'S READING:

....
....
....
....
....
....

Know Your Bible:

God blessed and performed miracles for the ancient Israelites, then had to discipline them for sinning. He lamented, "Oh, that my people had hearkened unto me!"

READ:
Psalms 78–82

Today's Date: _____

MY PRAYER FOR TODAY: ....
....
....

MY TAKEAWAY FROM TODAY'S READING:

....
....
....
....
....
....

Know Your Bible:

It is better to be a doorkeeper in God's temple than to live in "the tents of wickedness." The Lord loves Zion, Jerusalem, the "city of God."

READ:
Psalms 83–89

Today's Date: _____

MY PRAYER FOR TODAY: ....
....
....

Know Your Bible:

The human lifespan is seventy or eighty years, so Moses asked God to "teach us to number our days." It is good to thank God and sing His praises.

READ:
Psalms 90–99

MY TAKEAWAY FROM TODAY'S READING:

....
....
....
....
....
....

DAY 189

Today's Date: _____

MY PRAYER FOR TODAY: ....
....
....

Know Your Bible:

God's benefits include forgiving sins, healing diseases, and redeeming our lives from destruction. It is good to remember "his marvellous works."

READ:
Psalms 100–105

MY TAKEAWAY FROM TODAY'S READING:

....
....
....
....
....
....

DAY 190

Today's Date: _____

MY PRAYER FOR TODAY: ....
....
....

MY TAKEAWAY FROM TODAY'S READING:

....
....
....
....
....
....

Know Your Bible:

In spite of ancient Israel's many sinful failures, "many times did [God] deliver them." His mercy "is great above the heavens."

READ:
Psalms 106–109

Today's Date: _____

MY PRAYER FOR TODAY: ....
....
....

MY TAKEAWAY FROM
TODAY'S READING:

....
....
....
....
....
....

*Know
Your Bible:*

Praise, thanks, and love are
due the Lord by His people:
"Not unto us, but unto thy
name give glory, for thy mercy,
and for thy truth's sake."

READ:
Psalms 110–118

Today's Date: _____

MY PRAYER FOR TODAY: ....
....
....

*Know
Your Bible:*

The Bible's longest chapter
(176 verses) extols God's
Word, using names like "the
law of the LORD," "testimo-
nies," "precepts," "statutes,"
and "commandments."

READ:
Psalm 119

MY TAKEAWAY FROM
TODAY'S READING:

....
....
....
....
....
....

Today's Date: _____

MY PRAYER FOR TODAY: ....
....
....

Know Your Bible:

"Songs of degrees" were sung while going up to Jerusalem. When God's people trust in Him, they are "as mount Zion, which cannot be removed, but abideth for ever."

READ:
Psalms 120–134

MY TAKEAWAY FROM TODAY'S READING:
....
....
....
....
....
....

Today's Date: _____

MY PRAYER FOR TODAY: ....
....
....

MY TAKEAWAY FROM TODAY'S READING:
....
....
....
....
....
....

Know Your Bible:

God's mercy to His people endures forever, as do His knowledge of and thoughts toward them: "how great is the sum of them!"

READ:
Psalms 135–142

Today's Date: _____

MY PRAYER FOR TODAY: ....
....
....

MY TAKEAWAY FROM
TODAY'S READING:

....
....
....
....
....
....

*Know
Your Bible:*

People, angels, and all of creation are called to sing praise
to God. "Let every thing that
hath breath praise the Lord."

READ:
Psalms 143–150

Today's Date: _____

MY PRAYER FOR TODAY: ....
....
....

*Know
Your Bible:*

Solomon urges his sons to
search for wisdom "as for
hid treasures." The fear of
the Lord is the "beginning
of knowledge"; wise words
"are life unto those that find
them."

READ:
Proverbs 1–5

MY TAKEAWAY FROM
TODAY'S READING:

....
....
....
....
....
....

DAY 197

Today's Date: _____

MY PRAYER FOR TODAY: ....
....
....

Know Your Bible:

Laziness, pride, dishonesty, and adultery destroy people. Wisdom cries out for a hearing: "whoso findeth me findeth life, and shall obtain favour of the LORD."

READ:
Proverbs 6–9

MY TAKEAWAY FROM TODAY'S READING:

....
....
....
....
....
....

DAY 198

Today's Date: _____

MY PRAYER FOR TODAY: ....
....
....

MY TAKEAWAY FROM TODAY'S READING:

....
....
....
....
....
....

Know Your Bible:

Righteousness and wickedness stand in stark contrast: "Evil pursueth sinners: but to the righteous good shall be repayed."

READ:
Proverbs 10–14

Today's Date: _____ ▶ **DAY 199**

MY PRAYER FOR TODAY: ....
....
....

MY TAKEAWAY FROM TODAY'S READING:

....
....
....
....
....
....

Know Your Bible:

People must choose between good and evil: "The LORD is far from the wicked: but he heareth the prayer of the righteous."

READ: Proverbs 15–19

Today's Date: _____ ▶ **DAY 200**

MY PRAYER FOR TODAY: ....
....
....

Know Your Bible:

Wisdom offers warning: "wine is a mocker," "he that loveth pleasure shall be a poor man," "the borrower is servant to the lender," "make no friendship with an angry man."

READ: Proverbs 20–23

MY TAKEAWAY FROM TODAY'S READING:

....
....
....
....
....
....

DAY 201

Today's Date: _____

MY PRAYER FOR TODAY: ....
....
....

Know Your Bible:

Wisdom provides instruction: "a man of knowledge increaseth strength," "if thine enemy be hungry, give him bread to eat," "where there is no talebearer, the strife ceaseth."

READ:
Proverbs 24–28

MY TAKEAWAY FROM TODAY'S READING:

....
....
....
....
....
....

DAY 202

Today's Date: _____

MY PRAYER FOR TODAY: ....
....
....

MY TAKEAWAY FROM TODAY'S READING:

....
....
....
....
....
....

Know Your Bible:

The virtuous woman sets an example for everyone: "she looketh well to the ways of her household, and eateth not the bread of idleness."

READ:
Proverbs 29–31

Today's Date: _____

MY PRAYER FOR TODAY: ....
....
....

MY TAKEAWAY FROM
TODAY'S READING:

....
....
....
....
....
....

*Know
Your Bible:*

A "preacher, the son of
David, king in Jerusalem,"
seeks meaning in wealth and
pleasure, but finds "vanity"
and "vexation of spirit."

READ:
Ecclesiastes 1–6

Today's Date: _____

MY PRAYER FOR TODAY: ....
....
....

*Know
Your Bible:*

The Preacher realizes that on
earth, "all is vanity," so humanity's duty is to "fear God, and
keep his commandments."

READ:
Ecclesiastes 7–12

MY TAKEAWAY FROM
TODAY'S READING:

....
....
....
....
....
....

Today's Date: _____

MY PRAYER FOR TODAY: ....
....
....

Know Your Bible:

A handsome young king and his beautiful, dark-skinned bride celebrate their physical attraction and love for each other.

READ:
Song of Solomon 1–8

MY TAKEAWAY FROM TODAY'S READING:
....
....
....
....
....
....

Today's Date: _____

MY PRAYER FOR TODAY: ....
....
....

MY TAKEAWAY FROM TODAY'S READING:
....
....
....
....
....
....

Know Your Bible:

Isaiah, prophet to Judah during the reigns of Uzziah, Jotham, Ahaz, and Hezekiah, learns both of God's impending judgment and His blessing for the "last days."

READ:
Isaiah 1–4

Today's Date: _____

MY PRAYER FOR TODAY: ....

....

Know Your Bible:

Isaiah sees a powerful vision of God on His throne and carries the prophetic message of a virgin-born baby to be called Immanuel, or "God with Us."

READ:
Isaiah 5–7

MY TAKEAWAY FROM TODAY'S READING:

....

....

....

....

....

....

Today's Date: _____

MY PRAYER FOR TODAY: ....

....

Know Your Bible:

Prediction of Assyrian invasion is offset by the prophecy of the birth of a child called "Wonderful, Counsellor, The mighty God, The everlasting Father, The Prince of Peace."

READ:
Isaiah 8–10

MY TAKEAWAY FROM TODAY'S READING:

....

....

....

....

....

....

DAY 209

Today's Date: _____

MY PRAYER FOR TODAY: ....
....
....

Know Your Bible:

A future kingdom, built on God's promise to David, will see "the cow and bear" eating peacefully together. Before then, God will destroy power-ful Babylon.

READ:
Isaiah 11–14

MY TAKEAWAY FROM TODAY'S READING:

....
....
....
....
....
....

DAY 210

Today's Date: _____

MY PRAYER FOR TODAY: ....
....
....

MY TAKEAWAY FROM TODAY'S READING:

....
....
....
....
....
....

Know Your Bible:

God will judge and punish Moab, Damascus, and Egypt, but ultimately heal and draw many of these pagan people to Himself.

READ:
Isaiah 15–19

Today's Date: _____

MY PRAYER FOR TODAY: ....
....
....

MY TAKEAWAY FROM
TODAY'S READING:

....
....
....
....
....
....

*Know
Your Bible:*

Other warnings to pagan nations are accompanied by a prophecy of doom toward Jerusalem: "a day of trouble, and of treading down, and of perplexity by the Lord GOD."

READ:
Isaiah 20–23

Today's Date: _____

MY PRAYER FOR TODAY: ....
....
....

*Know
Your Bible:*

A coming judgment on the whole earth will be followed by a day when God "will swallow up death in victory" and "wipe away tears from off all faces."

READ:
Isaiah 24–27

MY TAKEAWAY FROM
TODAY'S READING:

....
....
....
....
....
....

Today's Date: _____

MY PRAYER FOR TODAY: ....
....
....

Know Your Bible:

Isaiah prophesies the Assyrian invasion of the northern kingdom of Israel and warns Judah against seeking military alliances with Egypt.

READ:
Isaiah 28–31

MY TAKEAWAY FROM TODAY'S READING:

....
....
....
....
....
....

Today's Date: _____

MY PRAYER FOR TODAY: ....
....
....

MY TAKEAWAY FROM TODAY'S READING:

....
....
....
....
....
....

Know Your Bible:

Isaiah looks ahead to the far future, when "a king shall reign in righteousness," God destroys all His enemies, and "the ransomed of the LORD" return to Jerusalem.

READ:
Isaiah 32–35

Today's Date: _____

MY PRAYER FOR TODAY: ....
....
....

MY TAKEAWAY FROM
TODAY'S READING:

....

....

....

....

....

....

*Know
Your Bible:*

Assyrians under Sennacherib
invade Judah. King Hezekiah
prays, Isaiah carries God's
message of victory, and the
angel of the Lord destroys
185,000 enemy soldiers.

READ:
Isaiah 36–39

Today's Date: _____

MY PRAYER FOR TODAY: ....
....
....

*Know
Your Bible:*

Isaiah proclaims prophecies
of John the Baptist ("him that
crieth in the wilderness") and
Jesus ("to open the blind eyes,
to bring out the prisoners
from the prison").

READ:
Isaiah 40–42

MY TAKEAWAY FROM
TODAY'S READING:

....

....

....

....

....

....

Today's Date: _____

MY PRAYER FOR TODAY: ....
....
....

Know Your Bible:

Judah faces captivity in Babylon, but Isaiah prophesies help from the Persian king Cyrus. However, it is in the Lord that "all the seed of Israel" will be justified.

READ:
Isaiah 43–45

MY TAKEAWAY FROM TODAY'S READING:

....
....
....
....
....
....

Today's Date: _____

MY PRAYER FOR TODAY: ....
....
....

MY TAKEAWAY FROM TODAY'S READING:

....
....
....
....
....
....

Know Your Bible:

God will judge Babylon for its arrogance, but the prideful Israelites will likewise face His punishment before being restored to their land.

READ:
Isaiah 46–48

Today's Date: _____ DAY 219

MY PRAYER FOR TODAY: ....
....
....

MY TAKEAWAY FROM
TODAY'S READING:

....
....
....
....
....
....

Know
Your Bible:

A coming Holy One, who will give His "back to the smiters," will redeem God's people, who will ultimately "come with singing unto Zion."

READ:
Isaiah 49–51

Today's Date: _____ DAY 220

MY PRAYER FOR TODAY: ....
....
....

Know
Your Bible:

The Holy One will be "wounded for our transgressions" and "bruised for our iniquities," bearing the sins of many and providing an everlasting salvation.

READ:
Isaiah 52–56

MY TAKEAWAY FROM
TODAY'S READING:

....
....
....
....
....
....

DAY 221

Today's Date: _____

MY PRAYER FOR TODAY: ....
....
....

Know Your Bible:

God's people are warned against idolatry, pride, empty forms of worship, and allowing or pursuing injustice against others.

READ:
Isaiah 57–59

MY TAKEAWAY FROM TODAY'S READING:
....
....
....
....
....
....

DAY 222

Today's Date: _____

MY PRAYER FOR TODAY: ....
....
....

MY TAKEAWAY FROM TODAY'S READING:
....
....
....
....
....
....

Know Your Bible:

A coming Deliverer will bring Jews and Gentiles together, and God will restore the devastated Jerusalem as "a crown of glory."

READ:
Isaiah 60–63

Today's Date: _____

MY PRAYER FOR TODAY: ....
....
....

MY TAKEAWAY FROM
TODAY'S READING:

....

....

....

....

....

....

*Know
Your Bible:*

God is planning "new heavens
and a new earth" where evil
people will be no more. It will
be a place of peace, comfort,
and flourishing.

READ:
Isaiah 64–66

Today's Date: _____

MY PRAYER FOR TODAY: ....
....
....

*Know
Your Bible:*

God calls young Jeremiah to
warn Judah of its backsliding, having "forsaken me the
fountain of living waters" and
committed spiritual adultery
with false gods.

READ:
Jeremiah 1–3

MY TAKEAWAY FROM
TODAY'S READING:

....

....

....

....

....

....

DAY 225

Today's Date: _____

MY PRAYER FOR TODAY: ....
....
....

Know Your Bible:

Judah is following false prophets and faithless priests. The nation's rebellion will result in an invasion by those who "are cruel, and have no mercy."

READ:
Jeremiah 4–6

MY TAKEAWAY FROM TODAY'S READING:

....
....
....
....
....
....

DAY 226

Today's Date: _____

MY PRAYER FOR TODAY: ....
....
....

MY TAKEAWAY FROM TODAY'S READING:

....
....
....
....
....
....

Know Your Bible:

Jeremiah preaches a message from the temple gate, calling out Judah's horrific practice of child sacrifice, among other sins.

READ:
Jeremiah 7–9

Today's Date: _____

MY PRAYER FOR TODAY: ....
....
....

MY TAKEAWAY FROM
TODAY'S READING:

....
....
....
....
....
....

*Know
Your Bible:*

Jeremiah points out that the
people have broken the covenant God gave them at Mount
Sinai. "Therefore," God says,
"I will bring evil upon them."

READ:
Jeremiah 10–12

Today's Date: _____

MY PRAYER FOR TODAY: ....
....
....

*Know
Your Bible:*

Jeremiah preaches on a devastating drought in Judah; it
will be followed by an enemy
invasion and the exile of many
people.

READ:
Jeremiah 13–15

MY TAKEAWAY FROM
TODAY'S READING:

....
....
....
....
....
....

Today's Date: _____

MY PRAYER FOR TODAY: ....
....
....

Know Your Bible:

God forbids Jeremiah to marry; his singleness represents Judah's estrangement from God. At a potter's house, Jeremiah learns that God fashions His people like clay.

READ:
Jeremiah 16–19

MY TAKEAWAY FROM TODAY'S READING:
....
....
....
....
....
....

Today's Date: _____

MY PRAYER FOR TODAY: ....
....
....

MY TAKEAWAY FROM TODAY'S READING:
....
....
....
....
....
....

Know Your Bible:

For his negative prophecies, Jeremiah is abused by other religious leaders. Jeremiah tells Zedekiah, Judah's last king, that he will fall into the hands of the Babylonians.

READ:
Jeremiah 20–22

Today's Date: _____

MY PRAYER FOR TODAY: ....
....
....

MY TAKEAWAY FROM
TODAY'S READING:

....
....
....
....
....
....

*Know
Your Bible:*

Jeremiah sees ahead to a "righteous Branch" from David's line, a king who will "execute judgment and justice in the earth." In the near term, Judah faces seventy years' captivity.

READ:
Jeremiah 23–25

Today's Date: _____

MY PRAYER FOR TODAY: ....
....
....

*Know
Your Bible:*

Jeremiah wears a yoke to tell King Zedekiah and Judah to "bring your necks under the yoke of the king of Babylon, and serve him and his people, and live."

READ:
Jeremiah 26–28

MY TAKEAWAY FROM
TODAY'S READING:

....
....
....
....
....
....

Today's Date: _____

MY PRAYER FOR TODAY: ....
....
....

Know Your Bible:

From Jerusalem, Jeremiah writes to Jewish leaders carried off to Babylon. They must seek the well-being of their new home, "for in the peace thereof shall ye have peace."

READ:
Jeremiah 29–30

MY TAKEAWAY FROM TODAY'S READING:

....
....
....
....
....
....

Today's Date: _____

MY PRAYER FOR TODAY: ....
....
....

MY TAKEAWAY FROM TODAY'S READING:

....
....
....
....
....
....

Know Your Bible:

God tells Jeremiah to purchase a field in Judah, despite the ongoing Babylonian siege. It is a sign that "houses and fields shall be possessed again in this land."

READ:
Jeremiah 31–32

Today's Date: _____

MY PRAYER FOR TODAY: ....
....
....

MY TAKEAWAY FROM TODAY'S READING:

....
....
....
....
....
....

Know Your Bible:

Jeremiah again prophesies of a future "Branch" of David who will rule righteously. In the near term, Jerusalem will fall to Babylon and King Zedekiah be captured.

READ:
Jeremiah 33–35

Today's Date: _____

MY PRAYER FOR TODAY: ....
....
....

Know Your Bible:

With Jerusalem under siege, Jeremiah is falsely accused of deserting and imprisoned. He urges the king to cooperate with the invaders, to limit damage to the city.

READ:
Jeremiah 36–38

MY TAKEAWAY FROM TODAY'S READING:

....
....
....
....
....
....

Today's Date: _____

MY PRAYER FOR TODAY: ....
....
....

Know Your Bible:

The Babylonians break through Jerusalem's walls, devastate the city, and carry its people into captivity. Jeremiah is allowed to stay and minister to the Jewish remnant.

READ:
Jeremiah 39–41

MY TAKEAWAY FROM TODAY'S READING:

....
....
....
....
....
....

Today's Date: _____

MY PRAYER FOR TODAY: ....
....
....

MY TAKEAWAY FROM TODAY'S READING:

....
....
....
....
....
....

Know Your Bible:

With the Babylonian-appointed governor of Judah assassinated, several leaders choose—against Jeremiah's counsel—to flee to Egypt. They force Jeremiah to join them.

READ:
Jeremiah 42–44

Today's Date: _____

MY PRAYER FOR TODAY: ....
....
....

MY TAKEAWAY FROM TODAY'S READING:

....
....
....
....
....
....

Know Your Bible:

Earlier prophecies against pagan nations are recounted, including one of the Babylonian king Nebuchadnezzar defeating Egypt's Pharaoh Necho in battle.

READ:
Jeremiah 45–47

Today's Date: _____

MY PRAYER FOR TODAY: ....
....
....

Know Your Bible:

Prophecies of judgment against Moab, Ammon, Edom, and Damascus are recorded.

READ:
Jeremiah 48–49

MY TAKEAWAY FROM TODAY'S READING:

....
....
....
....
....
....

DAY 241

MY PRAYER FOR TODAY: ....
....
....

Know Your Bible:

Babylon, which overran Judah and Jerusalem, will itself be conquered, and "all that spoil her will be satisfied."

READ:
Jeremiah 50

MY TAKEAWAY FROM TODAY'S READING:

....
....
....
....
....
....

DAY 242

MY PRAYER FOR TODAY: ....
....
....

MY TAKEAWAY FROM TODAY'S READING:

....
....
....
....
....
....

Know Your Bible:

Zedekiah rebels against the invaders, bringing destruction on Jerusalem. The temple is ransacked, and thousands of prominent citizens carried away into exile.

READ:
Jeremiah 51–52

Today's Date: _____   **DAY 243**

MY PRAYER FOR TODAY: ....
....
....

MY TAKEAWAY FROM
TODAY'S READING:

....
....
....
....
....
....

*Know
Your Bible:*

A series of sorrowful poems
mourns the destruction of
Jerusalem by the Babylonians.
"Jerusalem hath grievously
sinned," the writer says.
"Therefore she is removed."

READ:
Lamentations 1–2

Today's Date: _____   **DAY 244**

MY PRAYER FOR TODAY: ....
....
....

*Know
Your Bible:*

Amid crushing sorrow, Lamentations' author—perhaps
Jeremiah—recognizes that
"it is of the LORD's mercies we
are not consumed, because
his compassions fail not."

READ:
Lamentations 3–5

MY TAKEAWAY FROM
TODAY'S READING:

....
....
....
....
....
....

Today's Date: _____

MY PRAYER FOR TODAY: ....
....
....

Know Your Bible:

Ezekiel, a Jewish priest in Babylon, is called to be prophet to his fellow exiles. God calls Ezekiel "son of man," and sends him to an "impudent and hardhearted" people.

READ:
Ezekiel 1–3

MY TAKEAWAY FROM TODAY'S READING:

....
....
....
....
....
....

Today's Date: _____

MY PRAYER FOR TODAY: ....
....
....

MY TAKEAWAY FROM TODAY'S READING:

....
....
....
....
....
....

Know Your Bible:

Ezekiel performs symbolic acts—such as dividing his own hair into thirds, and burning, chopping, and scattering each part—to indicate the punishment coming on Jerusalem.

READ:
Ezekiel 4–7

MY PRAYER FOR TODAY: ....
....
....

MY TAKEAWAY FROM
TODAY'S READING:

....
....
....
....
....
....

*Know
Your Bible:*

In a vision, Ezekiel sees six
angelic executioners destroying everyone in Jerusalem
except those who mourned
over the city's sin.

READ:
Ezekiel 8–11

MY PRAYER FOR TODAY: ....
....
....

*Know
Your Bible:*

Ezekiel continues to act out
prophecies, including digging
through a wall to exit his own
house, a symbol of the coming
Babylonian invasion and exile.

READ:
Ezekiel 12–15

MY TAKEAWAY FROM
TODAY'S READING:

....
....
....
....
....
....

Today's Date: _____

MY PRAYER FOR TODAY: ....
....
....

Know Your Bible:

Jerusalem is accused of harlotry for pursuing false gods and even burning children in sacrifice. Even so, Ezekiel describes a future day when Israel will again honor God.

READ:
Ezekiel 16–17

MY TAKEAWAY FROM TODAY'S READING:

....
....
....
....
....
....

Today's Date: _____

MY PRAYER FOR TODAY: ....
....
....

MY TAKEAWAY FROM TODAY'S READING:

....
....
....
....
....
....

Know Your Bible:

Through Ezekiel, God teaches individual responsibility: "The soul that sinneth, it shall die." And God takes no pleasure in anyone's death: "Turn yourselves, and live."

READ:
Ezekiel 18–20

Today's Date: _____

MY PRAYER FOR TODAY: ....
....
....

MY TAKEAWAY FROM TODAY'S READING:

....
....
....
....
....
....

Know Your Bible:

God accuses His people of bloodshed, robbery, and oppression: "Therefore have I poured out my indignation upon them."

READ:
Ezekiel 21–22

Today's Date: _____

MY PRAYER FOR TODAY: ....
....
....

Know Your Bible:

God describes Israel and Judah as two sisters who engage in prostitution. As a sign to the people, Ezekiel is forbidden to publicly mourn when his wife dies.

READ:
Ezekiel 23–24

MY TAKEAWAY FROM TODAY'S READING:

....
....
....
....
....
....

Today's Date: _____

MY PRAYER FOR TODAY: ....

....

....

Know Your Bible:

Ezekiel delivers pronouncements of God's judgment on the surrounding nations of Ammon, Moab, Edom, Philistia, and Tyre for their many sins.

READ:
Ezekiel 25–27

MY TAKEAWAY FROM TODAY'S READING:

....

....

....

....

....

....

Today's Date: _____

MY PRAYER FOR TODAY: ....

....

....

MY TAKEAWAY FROM TODAY'S READING:

....

....

....

....

....

....

Know Your Bible:

The king of Tyre is denounced for his pride in language that seems to describe Satan's origins. A future regathering of Israel is again mentioned.

READ:
Ezekiel 28–30

Today's Date: _____ DAY 255

MY PRAYER FOR TODAY:
....
....
....

MY TAKEAWAY FROM TODAY'S READING:
....
....
....
....
....
....

Know Your Bible:

Ezekiel prophesies God's judgment on Egypt and the pharaoh. The Lord will use "the sword of the king of Babylon."

READ:
Ezekiel 31–32

Today's Date: _____ DAY 256

MY PRAYER FOR TODAY:
....
....
....

Know Your Bible:

God criticizes Israel's "shepherds" (kings) for their selfishness and oppression of the people, promising someday to install "one shepherd over them. . .even my servant David."

READ:
Ezekiel 33–34

MY TAKEAWAY FROM TODAY'S READING:
....
....
....
....
....
....

Today's Date: _____

MY PRAYER FOR TODAY: ....
....
....

Know Your Bible:

God promises to restore Israel "for mine holy name's sake," even though their behavior had profaned Him before the nations.

READ:
Ezekiel 35–36

MY TAKEAWAY FROM TODAY'S READING:

....
....
....
....
....
....

Today's Date: _____

MY PRAYER FOR TODAY: ....
....
....

MY TAKEAWAY FROM TODAY'S READING:

....
....
....
....
....
....

Know Your Bible:

Ezekiel has a vision of a valley full of dry bones which are restored to life, a symbol of the future restoration of God's people.

READ:
Ezekiel 37–39

Today's Date: _____ DAY 259

MY PRAYER FOR TODAY: ....
....
....

MY TAKEAWAY FROM
TODAY'S READING:

....
....
....
....
....
....

*Know
Your Bible:*

Twenty-five years into their
captivity, Ezekiel sees a vision
of a beautiful future temple
of God.

READ:
Ezekiel 40–42

Today's Date: _____ DAY 260

MY PRAYER FOR TODAY: ....
....
....

*Know
Your Bible:*

In his vision, Ezekiel witnesses
God's glory filling the temple.
God describes His expecta-
tions for the priests who serve
in the temple.

READ:
Ezekiel 43–44

MY TAKEAWAY FROM
TODAY'S READING:

....
....
....
....
....
....

DAY 261

Today's Date: _____

MY PRAYER FOR TODAY: ....
....
....

Know Your Bible:

Worship practices in the future temple—offerings and celebrations—are defined.

READ:
Ezekiel 45–46

MY TAKEAWAY FROM TODAY'S READING:

....
....
....
....
....
....

DAY 262

Today's Date: _____

MY PRAYER FOR TODAY: ....
....
....

MY TAKEAWAY FROM TODAY'S READING:

....
....
....
....
....
....

Know Your Bible:

Ezekiel describes a river issuing from the future temple, feeding numerous trees on its banks and healing the Dead Sea. The name of the city becomes, "The LORD is there."

READ:
Ezekiel 47–48

Today's Date: _____

MY PRAYER FOR TODAY: ....
....
....

MY TAKEAWAY FROM
TODAY'S READING:

....

....

....

....

....

....

*Know
Your Bible:*

Daniel and three friends are
among promising young
Jews taken into the service
of conquering Babylon. He
interprets the king's dreams
and is promoted to leadership.

READ:
Daniel 1–2

Today's Date: _____

MY PRAYER FOR TODAY: ....
....
....

*Know
Your Bible:*

Babylon's king, Nebuchadnezzar, orders all people to worship a golden statue. Daniel's
three friends refuse and are
thrown into a burning furnace.
God rescues them.

READ:
Daniel 3–4

MY TAKEAWAY FROM
TODAY'S READING:

....

....

....

....

....

....

DAY 265

MY PRAYER FOR TODAY: ....
....
....

Know Your Bible:

Under the Persian king Darius, Daniel is thrown into a den of lions for praying to God. God rescues him.

READ:
Daniel 5–6

MY TAKEAWAY FROM TODAY'S READING:
....
....
....
....
....
....

DAY 266

Today's Date: _____

MY PRAYER FOR TODAY: ....
....
....

MY TAKEAWAY FROM TODAY'S READING:
....
....
....
....
....
....

Know Your Bible:

Daniel has visions of coming world kingdoms, the end times, and "the Son of man" coming in the clouds, who will rule with "everlasting dominion."

READ:
Daniel 7–9

Today's Date: _____   **DAY 267**

MY PRAYER FOR TODAY: ....
....
....

MY TAKEAWAY FROM TODAY'S READING:

....
....
....
....
....
....

Know Your Bible:

Daniel tells of end-times events, culminating in a "time of trouble" followed by the resurrection of "some to everlasting life and some to shame and everlasting contempt."

READ:
Daniel 10–12

Today's Date: _____   **DAY 268**

MY PRAYER FOR TODAY: ....
....
....

Know Your Bible:

God tells Hosea to take "a wife of whoredoms" to picture His own relationship with adulterous Israel. Then Hosea is to pursue his straying wife as God pursues His people.

READ:
Hosea 1–5

MY TAKEAWAY FROM TODAY'S READING:

....
....
....
....
....
....

Today's Date: _____

MY PRAYER FOR TODAY: ....
....
....

Know Your Bible:

God calls out the northern kingdom's wickedness and trust in other nations rather than Him. "Ye have plowed wickedness," He tells them; "ye have reaped iniquity."

READ:
Hosea 6–10

MY TAKEAWAY FROM TODAY'S READING:
....
....
....
....
....
....

Today's Date: _____

MY PRAYER FOR TODAY: ....
....
....

MY TAKEAWAY FROM TODAY'S READING:
....
....
....
....
....
....

Know Your Bible:

Israel will become subject to the vicious Assyrians, but God will ultimately "heal their backsliding" and "love them freely."

READ:
Hosea 11–14

Today's Date: _____

MY PRAYER FOR TODAY: ....
....
....

MY TAKEAWAY FROM
TODAY'S READING:

....
....
....
....
....
....

*Know
Your Bible:*

Locusts devastate the land,
and Joel uses this disaster as
a picture of God's coming
judgment for His people's sin.
But one day He will "pour out
[His] spirit upon all flesh."

READ:
Joel 1–3

Today's Date: _____

MY PRAYER FOR TODAY: ....
....
....

*Know
Your Bible:*

God calls a shepherd as prophet to both Israel and Judah
in their times of prosperity.
Amos chastises them, among
other things, for their oppression of the poor.

READ:
Amos 1–5

MY TAKEAWAY FROM
TODAY'S READING:

....
....
....
....
....
....

Today's Date: _____

MY PRAYER FOR TODAY: ....
....
....

Know Your Bible:

Amos warns God's people that they will be carried off by enemies; Obadiah pronounces doom on the enemy nation of Edom. "But upon mount Zion shall be deliverance."

READ:
Amos 6–9; Obadiah

MY TAKEAWAY FROM TODAY'S READING:

....
....
....
....
....
....

Today's Date: _____

MY PRAYER FOR TODAY: ....
....
....

MY TAKEAWAY FROM TODAY'S READING:

....
....
....
....
....
....

Know Your Bible:

A reluctant prophet tries to avoid preaching to the wicked city of Nineveh; God forces the issue with Jonah, he obeys, and the pagan people repent.

READ:
Jonah 1–4

Today's Date: _____

MY PRAYER FOR TODAY: ....
....
....

MY TAKEAWAY FROM
TODAY'S READING:

....
....
....
....
....
....

*Know
Your Bible:*

Micah prophesies trouble for God's sinful people, but also the exact birthplace of the coming Messiah: Bethlehem in Judah.

READ:
Micah 1–7

Today's Date: _____

MY PRAYER FOR TODAY: ....
....
....

*Know
Your Bible:*

Nahum speaks doom on the "bloody city" of Nineveh, capital of Assyria. Habakkuk asks how God can use "bitter and hasty" Chaldeans (Babylonians) for His purposes.

READ:
Nahum 1–3;
Habakkuk 1–3

MY TAKEAWAY FROM
TODAY'S READING:

....
....
....
....
....
....

DAY 277

Today's Date: _____

MY PRAYER FOR TODAY: ....
....
....

Know Your Bible:

Zephaniah warns sinful Jerusalem of judgment but promises a future blessing. Haggai demands that the Jews returned from exile finish their work on God's temple.

READ:
Zephaniah 1–3;
Haggai 1–2

MY TAKEAWAY FROM TODAY'S READING:

....
....
....
....
....
....

DAY 278

Today's Date: _____

MY PRAYER FOR TODAY: ....
....
....

MY TAKEAWAY FROM TODAY'S READING:

....
....
....
....
....
....

Know Your Bible:

A prophet and priest after the exile, Zechariah describes a day when God will come and "dwell in the midst" of His people.

READ:
Zechariah 1–4

Today's Date: _____ **DAY 279**

MY PRAYER FOR TODAY: ....
....
....

MY TAKEAWAY FROM TODAY'S READING:

....
....
....
....
....
....

Know Your Bible:

Zechariah's forward-looking prophecies include one of a King entering Jerusalem "lowly, and riding upon an ass, and upon a colt the foal of an ass."

READ:
Zechariah 5–9

Today's Date: _____ **DAY 280**

MY PRAYER FOR TODAY: ....
....
....

Know Your Bible:

An end-times battle in which God "will gather all nations against Jerusalem" will be followed by a day when "the LORD shall be king over all the earth."

READ:
Zechariah 10–14

MY TAKEAWAY FROM TODAY'S READING:

....
....
....
....
....
....

DAY 281 — Today's Date: _____

MY PRAYER FOR TODAY: ....
....
....

Know Your Bible:

Malachi challenges the returned exiles to observe their duties before God; in the more distant future, "the Sun of righteousness" will arise "with healing in his wings."

READ:
Malachi 1–4

MY TAKEAWAY FROM TODAY'S READING:
....
....
....
....
....

DAY 282 — Today's Date: _____

MY PRAYER FOR TODAY: ....
....
....

MY TAKEAWAY FROM TODAY'S READING:
....
....
....
....
....
....

Know Your Bible:

Jesus is born in the family line of David, baptized by His precursor John, and tempted by Satan. He calls disciples and begins His ministry in Capernaum of Galilee.

READ:
Matthew 1–4

Today's Date: _____

MY PRAYER FOR TODAY: ....
....
....

MY TAKEAWAY FROM
TODAY'S READING:

....
....
....
....
....
....

*Know
Your Bible:*

In the "sermon on the Mount,"
Jesus says He did not come
"to destroy the law, or the
prophets," but to fulfill them.

READ:
Matthew 5–7

Today's Date: _____

MY PRAYER FOR TODAY: ....
....
....

*Know
Your Bible:*

Jesus proves His power by
healing diseases, casting
out demons, controlling the
weather, and raising the dead.
He calls the tax collector
Matthew as a disciple.

READ:
Matthew 8–9

MY TAKEAWAY FROM
TODAY'S READING:

....
....
....
....
....

DAY 285

Today's Date: _____

MY PRAYER FOR TODAY: ....
....
....

Know Your Bible:

Jesus' twelve disciples are sent out to preach to "the lost sheep of the house of Israel." He offers rest to those "that labour and are heavy laden."

READ:
Matthew 10–11

MY TAKEAWAY FROM TODAY'S READING:

....
....
....
....
....
....

DAY 286

Today's Date: _____

MY PRAYER FOR TODAY: ....
....
....

MY TAKEAWAY FROM TODAY'S READING:

....
....
....
....
....
....

Know Your Bible:

Jesus declares Himself "Lord even of the sabbath day"; hints of His coming death and resurrection; and teaches of the kingdom of heaven in parables.

READ:
Matthew 12–13

Today's Date: _____

MY PRAYER FOR TODAY: ....

....

....

MY TAKEAWAY FROM
TODAY'S READING:

....

....

....

....

....

....

*Know
Your Bible:*

Jesus miraculously feeds
crowds of four- and five thousand people, then steps up
His criticism of the Jewish
religious leaders, the scribes
and Pharisees.

READ:
Matthew 14–16

Today's Date: _____

MY PRAYER FOR TODAY: ....

....

....

*Know
Your Bible:*

The disciples Peter, James,
and John witness Jesus' true
glory during His transfigu-
ration; Jesus speaks plainly
of His coming death and
resurrection.

READ:
Matthew 17–19

MY TAKEAWAY FROM
TODAY'S READING:

....

....

....

....

....

....

Today's Date: _____

MY PRAYER FOR TODAY: ....
....
....

Know Your Bible:

Jesus details His impending crucifixion. He tells Jewish leaders, "The kingdom of God shall be taken from you, and given to a nation bringing forth the fruits thereof."

READ:
Matthew 20–21

MY TAKEAWAY FROM TODAY'S READING:

....
....
....
....
....
....

Today's Date: _____

MY PRAYER FOR TODAY: ....
....
....

MY TAKEAWAY FROM TODAY'S READING:

....
....
....
....
....
....

Know Your Bible:

Jesus quiets the Pharisees with His questions, then pronounces woe upon them: "For ye shut up the kingdom of heaven against men."

READ:
Matthew 22–23

Today's Date: _____

MY PRAYER FOR TODAY: ·····································
···
···

MY TAKEAWAY FROM
TODAY'S READING:

··
··
··
··
··
··

Know Your Bible:

In His "Olivet Discourse," Jesus describes the sad state of the world before His second coming, and His ultimate separating of the good from the wicked.

READ:
Matthew 24–25

Today's Date: _____

MY PRAYER FOR TODAY: ·····································
···
···

Know Your Bible:

Judas Iscariot agrees to betray Jesus to Jewish leaders. Jesus has His last supper with the disciples, then prays at Gethsemane. He is arrested, and His disciples flee.

READ:
Matthew 26

MY TAKEAWAY FROM
TODAY'S READING:

··
··
··
··
··
··

Today's Date: _____

MY PRAYER FOR TODAY: ....

....

....

Know Your Bible:

Jesus is falsely accused, mocked, crucified, and buried. On the third day, angels announce, "He is risen." Jesus tells His followers to "teach all nations" about Him.

READ:
Matthew 27–28

MY TAKEAWAY FROM TODAY'S READING:

....

....

....

....

....

....

Today's Date: _____

MY PRAYER FOR TODAY: ....

....

....

MY TAKEAWAY FROM TODAY'S READING:

....

....

....

....

....

....

Know Your Bible:

John the Baptist prepares the way for Jesus, who calls disciples, heals the sick, and says whoever does God's will is "my brother, and my sister, and mother."

READ:
Mark 1–3

Today's Date: _____ | DAY 295

MY PRAYER FOR TODAY: ···
··
··

MY TAKEAWAY FROM
TODAY'S READING:

·······································
·······································
·······································
·······································
·······································
·······································

*Know
Your Bible:*

Jesus teaches in parables,
drives numerous demons
from a man called Legion,
raises a nobleman's daughter from the dead, and walks
on the stormy Sea of Galilee.

READ:
Mark 4–6

Today's Date: _____ | DAY 296

MY PRAYER FOR TODAY: ···
··
··

*Know
Your Bible:*

Jesus rebukes the hypocritical
Pharisees, extends His blessing to a non-Jewish woman,
and is transfigured. Peter recognizes Jesus as the Christ, or
Messiah, the Jews anticipate.

READ:
Mark 7–9

MY TAKEAWAY FROM
TODAY'S READING:

·······································
·······································
·······································
·······································
·······································
·······································

DAY 297

Today's Date: _____

MY PRAYER FOR TODAY: ....
....
....

Know Your Bible:

Jesus rides into Jerusalem on a donkey, fulfilling a prophecy of Zechariah. The chief priests and scribes and elders of Israel question His authority.

READ:
Mark 10–11

MY TAKEAWAY FROM TODAY'S READING:

....
....
....
....
....
....

DAY 298

Today's Date: _____

MY PRAYER FOR TODAY: ....
....
....

MY TAKEAWAY FROM TODAY'S READING:

....
....
....
....
....
....

Know Your Bible:

Jesus identifies the greatest commandment in the law as, "Love the Lord thy God with all thy heart, and with all thy soul, and with all thy mind, and with all thy strength."

READ:
Mark 12–13

Today's Date: _____ DAY 299

MY PRAYER FOR TODAY: ....
....
....

MY TAKEAWAY FROM
TODAY'S READING:

....
....
....
....
....
....

*Know
Your Bible:*

Jesus is arrested, and Peter
fearfully denies knowing Him.
Jesus dies on a cross, is buried,
and rises again. He tells His
disciples, "Go ye into all the
world, and preach the gospel."

READ:
Mark 14–16

Today's Date: _____ DAY 300

MY PRAYER FOR TODAY: ....
....
....

*Know
Your Bible:*

Luke compiles eyewitness ac-
counts of the life and ministry
of Jesus, beginning with His
miraculous conception and
the birth of His relative John
the Baptist.

READ:
Luke 1

MY TAKEAWAY FROM
TODAY'S READING:

....
....
....
....
....
....

Today's Date: _____

MY PRAYER FOR TODAY: ....
....
....

Know Your Bible:

Jesus is born to the virgin Mary in Bethlehem, then dedicated at the temple. Years later, at about age thirty, He is baptized by John and begins His public ministry.

READ:
Luke 2–3

MY TAKEAWAY FROM TODAY'S READING:

....
....
....
....
....
....

Today's Date: _____

MY PRAYER FOR TODAY: ....
....
....

MY TAKEAWAY FROM TODAY'S READING:

....
....
....
....
....
....

Know Your Bible:

Jesus defeats Satan's temptation in the wilderness. Then, in the Nazareth synagogue, He announces Himself as the fulfillment of Isaiah's prophecy.

READ:
Luke 4–5

Today's Date: _____

MY PRAYER FOR TODAY: ....
....
....

MY TAKEAWAY FROM
TODAY'S READING:

....
....
....
....
....
....

*Know
Your Bible:*

Luke records a shortened
version of Jesus' sermon on
the mount and describes
His healing of a Roman centurion's servant.

READ:
Luke 6–7

Today's Date: _____

MY PRAYER FOR TODAY: ....
....
....

*Know
Your Bible:*

Jesus preaches and heals
throughout Galilee, then stills
a storm on the sea. He sends
His twelve disciples out to
preach, and is transfigured before Peter, James, and John.

READ:
Luke 8–9

MY TAKEAWAY FROM
TODAY'S READING:

....
....
....
....
....
....

DAY 305

Today's Date: _____

MY PRAYER FOR TODAY: ....
....
....

Know Your Bible:

Jesus sends seventy other followers out to preach. He speaks the parable of the good Samaritan and mentions "the sign of Jonas"—the three days He will spend in the grave.

READ:
Luke 10–11

MY TAKEAWAY FROM TODAY'S READING:

....
....
....
....
....
....

DAY 306

Today's Date: _____

MY PRAYER FOR TODAY: ....
....
....

MY TAKEAWAY FROM TODAY'S READING:

....
....
....
....
....
....

Know Your Bible:

Jesus warns of the Pharisees' hypocritical ways, acknowledges that He will divide family members, and calls all people to repent.

READ:
Luke 12–13

Today's Date: _____

MY PRAYER FOR TODAY: ....
....
....

MY TAKEAWAY FROM
TODAY'S READING:

....
....
....
....
....
....

*Know
Your Bible:*

Jesus heals a diseased man
on the sabbath, then tells
the grumbling Pharisees the
parable of the lost son—God
welcomes the humble, any
who "was lost, and is found."

READ:
Luke 14–15

Today's Date: _____

MY PRAYER FOR TODAY: ....
....
....

*Know
Your Bible:*

Jesus' story of the rich man
and Lazarus warns of hell; He
commands forgiveness to
anyone who asks; and He tells
of His second coming.

READ:
Luke 16–17

MY TAKEAWAY FROM
TODAY'S READING:

....
....
....
....
....
....

Today's Date: _____

MY PRAYER FOR TODAY: ....
....
....

*Know
Your Bible:*

Jesus blesses little children;
heals a blind man; welcomes
the tax collector Zacchaeus
into God's kingdom; and
makes His triumphal entry
into Jerusalem.

READ:
Luke 18–19

MY TAKEAWAY FROM
TODAY'S READING:

....
....
....
....
....
....

Today's Date: _____

MY PRAYER FOR TODAY: ....
....
....

MY TAKEAWAY FROM
TODAY'S READING:

....
....
....
....
....
....

*Know
Your Bible:*

Jesus answers the Pharisees'
trick question on taxes by saying, "Render therefore unto
Caesar the things which be
Caesar's, and unto God the
things which be God's."

READ:
Luke 20:1–22:38

Today's Date: _____

MY PRAYER FOR TODAY: ....
....
....

MY TAKEAWAY FROM
TODAY'S READING:

....
....
....
....
....
....

Know
Your Bible:

On the cross, Jesus welcomes a repentant thief into God's kingdom. After His resurrection, He meets several times with His disciples, to help them "understand the scriptures."

READ:
Luke 22:39–24:53

Today's Date: _____

MY PRAYER FOR TODAY: ....
....
....

Know
Your Bible:

Jesus is "the Word," who is God, and through whom the world was made. He promises that whoever believes in Him "should not perish, but have everlasting life."

READ:
John 1–3

MY TAKEAWAY FROM
TODAY'S READING:

....
....
....
....
....
....

Today's Date: _____

MY PRAYER FOR TODAY: ....
....
....

Know Your Bible:

Jesus tells a Samaritan woman that He is the Messiah; He tells the Jewish leaders, "I seek not mine own will, but the will of the Father which hath sent me."

READ:
John 4–5

MY TAKEAWAY FROM TODAY'S READING:

....
....
....
....
....
....
....

Today's Date: _____

MY PRAYER FOR TODAY: ....
....
....

MY TAKEAWAY FROM TODAY'S READING:

....
....
....
....
....
....

Know Your Bible:

Jesus feeds five thousand people with a boy's lunch and calls Himself "the bread which came down from heaven." Peter calls Jesus "the Christ, the Son of the living God."

READ:
John 6–7

Today's Date: _____

MY PRAYER FOR TODAY: ....
....
....

MY TAKEAWAY FROM
TODAY'S READING:

....
....
....
....
....
....

**Know
Your Bible:**

Jesus protects a woman
caught in the act of adultery
and calls Himself "the light
of the world." He heals a man
born blind, setting off more
conflict with the Pharisees.

READ:
John 8–9

Today's Date: _____

MY PRAYER FOR TODAY: ....
....
....

**Know
Your Bible:**

Jesus describes Himself as the
good shepherd who "giveth
his life for the sheep." He
asserts His deity: "I and my
Father are one." Jesus raises
Lazarus from the dead.

READ:
John 10–11

MY TAKEAWAY FROM
TODAY'S READING:

....
....
....
....
....
....

Today's Date: _____

MY PRAYER FOR TODAY: ....
....
....

Know Your Bible:

Jesus is hailed as king in His triumphal entry into Jerusalem. He eats His last supper with the disciples and foretells His betrayal by Judas Iscariot.

READ:
John 12–13

MY TAKEAWAY FROM TODAY'S READING:

....
....
....
....
....
....

Today's Date: _____

MY PRAYER FOR TODAY: ....
....
....

MY TAKEAWAY FROM TODAY'S READING:

....
....
....
....
....
....

Know Your Bible:

Jesus warns His followers that they will experience persecution but promises He will "prepare a place" for them and send them "another Comforter," the Holy Spirit.

READ:
John 14–16

Today's Date: _____

MY PRAYER FOR TODAY: ....
....
....

MY TAKEAWAY FROM
TODAY'S READING:

....
....
....
....
....
....

Know Your Bible:

Jesus prays for His disciples, and for all who will believe in Him through their preaching. He is arrested, denied by Peter, and tried before the Roman governor Pilate.

READ:
John 17–18

Today's Date: _____

MY PRAYER FOR TODAY: ....
....
....

Know Your Bible:

Jesus dies on a cross, saying, "It is finished," but returns to life on the third day. He restores Peter, telling him, "Feed my sheep."

READ:
John 19–21

MY TAKEAWAY FROM
TODAY'S READING:

....
....
....
....
....
....

Today's Date: _____

MY PRAYER FOR TODAY: ....

....

....

Know Your Bible:

Forty days after His resurrection, Jesus ascends into heaven. On Pentecost, the Holy Spirit comes to believers. Peter preaches in Jerusalem, and three thousand are saved.

READ:
Acts 1–2

MY TAKEAWAY FROM TODAY'S READING:

....

....

....

....

....

....

Today's Date: _____

MY PRAYER FOR TODAY: ....

....

....

MY TAKEAWAY FROM TODAY'S READING:

....

....

....

....

....

....

Know Your Bible:

Peter and John heal a lame man in Jesus' name, bringing persecution on the believers. A couple in the early church dies after dishonestly presenting an offering.

READ:
Acts 3–5

DAY 323

MY PRAYER FOR TODAY: ....
....
....

MY TAKEAWAY FROM TODAY'S READING:

....
....
....
....
....
....

Know Your Bible:

Deacons are chosen to help with the administration of the early church. One of them, Stephen, is martyred for his strong preaching to the Jewish ruling council.

READ:
Acts 6–7

DAY 324

MY PRAYER FOR TODAY: ....
....
....

Know Your Bible:

A leader of the persecution, Saul, is converted by the direct intervention of Jesus. Barnabas, a faithful Christian, convinces other believers to accept their former enemy.

READ:
Acts 8–9

MY TAKEAWAY FROM TODAY'S READING:

....
....
....
....
....
....

Today's Date: _____

MY PRAYER FOR TODAY: ....
....
....

Know Your Bible:

God extends salvation to the Gentiles by having Peter share the Gospel with the centurion Cornelius. Christians fleeing persecution take the message to other regions.

READ:
Acts 10–12

MY TAKEAWAY FROM TODAY'S READING:

....
....
....
....
....
....

Today's Date: _____

MY PRAYER FOR TODAY: ....
....
....

MY TAKEAWAY FROM TODAY'S READING:

....
....
....
....
....
....

Know Your Bible:

In Antioch, where believers were first called "Christians," God separates Saul and Barnabas for missionary service. Saul becomes known as Paul.

READ:
Acts 13–14

Today's Date: _____

MY PRAYER FOR TODAY: ....
....
....

MY TAKEAWAY FROM
TODAY'S READING:

....
....
....
....
....
....

*Know
Your Bible:*

Jesus' apostles announce
that Christians do not need
to observe Jewish rituals such
as circumcision. Paul begins
a second missionary jour-
ney, through Asia Minor and
Greece.

READ:
Acts 15–17

Today's Date: _____

MY PRAYER FOR TODAY: ....
....
....

*Know
Your Bible:*

Paul spends eighteen months
in Corinth, facing Jewish op-
position. In Ephesus, silver-
smiths riot over his message,
which they fear hurts their
idol-making business.

READ:
Acts 18–19

MY TAKEAWAY FROM
TODAY'S READING:

....
....
....
....
....
....

DAY 329

MY PRAYER FOR TODAY: ....
....
....

Know Your Bible:

Paul returns to Jerusalem, where his opponents stir up a riot. Roman soldiers intervene and allow Paul to defend himself before the crowd. The people call for Paul's death.

READ:
Acts 20–22

MY TAKEAWAY FROM TODAY'S READING:

....
....
....
....
....
....

DAY 330

MY PRAYER FOR TODAY: ....
....
....

MY TAKEAWAY FROM TODAY'S READING:

....
....
....
....
....
....

Know Your Bible:

Paul appears before the Sanhedrin (Jewish ruling council), then before the Roman leaders Felix and Festus, all without resolution. A Roman citizen, he appeals to Caesar.

READ:
Acts 23–25

Today's Date: _____

MY PRAYER FOR TODAY: ....
....
....

MY TAKEAWAY FROM TODAY'S READING:

....
....
....
....
....
....

Know Your Bible:

On his way to Rome, Paul survives shipwreck and a venomous snake bite on the shore of Malta. Acts ends with Paul in Rome, preaching and teaching from a rented house.

READ:
Acts 26–28

Today's Date: _____

MY PRAYER FOR TODAY: ....
....
....

Know Your Bible:

To believers in Rome, Paul explains humanity's guilt before God, which can only be corrected by faith in Jesus Christ.

READ:
Romans 1–3

MY TAKEAWAY FROM TODAY'S READING:

....
....
....
....
....
....

DAY 333

Today's Date: _____

MY PRAYER FOR TODAY: ....
....
....

Know Your Bible:

Justification by faith leads to "peace with God through our Lord Jesus Christ." Believers must consider themselves dead to sin, but alive to God through Jesus.

READ:
Romans 4–7

MY TAKEAWAY FROM TODAY'S READING:

....
....
....
....
....
....

DAY 334

Today's Date: _____

MY PRAYER FOR TODAY: ....
....
....

MY TAKEAWAY FROM TODAY'S READING:

....
....
....
....
....
....

Know Your Bible:

For those who are "in Christ Jesus," there is no condemnation for sin. Nothing—tribulation, distress, persecution, famine, or sword—can separate us from His love.

READ:
Romans 8–10

Today's Date: _____

MY PRAYER FOR TODAY: ....
....
....

MY TAKEAWAY FROM
TODAY'S READING:

....
....
....
....
....
....

*Know
Your Bible:*

Christians should offer themselves to God as "living sacri-
fices," renewing their minds
and not being "conformed to
this world."

READ:
Romans 11–13

Today's Date: _____

MY PRAYER FOR TODAY: ....
....
....

*Know
Your Bible:*

Christians enjoy great free-
dom from religious rules, but
should honor the beliefs of
others, bearing "the infirmi-
ties of the weak, and not to
please ourselves."

READ:
Romans 14–16

MY TAKEAWAY FROM
TODAY'S READING:

....
....
....
....
....
....

Today's Date: _____

MY PRAYER FOR TODAY: ....
....
....

Know Your Bible:

The apostle Paul chides the Corinthian church for allowing (even celebrating) an immoral relationship in their fellowship, as well as for taking each other to court.

READ:
1 Corinthians 1–6

MY TAKEAWAY FROM TODAY'S READING:

....
....
....
....
....
....
....

Today's Date: _____

MY PRAYER FOR TODAY: ....
....
....

MY TAKEAWAY FROM TODAY'S READING:

....
....
....
....
....
....

Know Your Bible:

Paul defends his apostleship to the Corinthians, warns them from Israel's history, and says, "whatsoever ye do, do all to the glory of God."

READ:
1 Corinthians 7–10

Today's Date: _____   **DAY 339**

MY PRAYER FOR TODAY: ....
....
....

MY TAKEAWAY FROM TODAY'S READING:

....
....
....
....
....
....

Know Your Bible:

Paul describes the variety of spiritual gifts that God gives Christians, urges their use to the benefit of "the body of Christ," and commends love as the motive of all.

READ:
1 Corinthians 11–13

Today's Date: _____   **DAY 340**

MY PRAYER FOR TODAY: ....
....
....

Know Your Bible:

Jesus' resurrection is a sign that all who follow Him will be raised to eternal life: "this corruptible must put on incorruption, and this mortal must put on immortality."

READ:
1 Corinthians 14–16

MY TAKEAWAY FROM TODAY'S READING:

....
....
....
....
....
....

DAY 341

Today's Date: _____

MY PRAYER FOR TODAY: ....
....
....

Know Your Bible:

The Gospel ministry brings with it heavy burdens, but Paul says, "we have this treasure in earthen vessels, that the excellency of the power may be of God, and not of us."

READ:
2 Corinthians 1–5

MY TAKEAWAY FROM TODAY'S READING:

....
....
....
....
....
....

DAY 342

Today's Date: _____

MY PRAYER FOR TODAY: ....
....
....

MY TAKEAWAY FROM TODAY'S READING:

....
....
....
....
....
....

Know Your Bible:

Paul urges the Corinthians to give toward an offering for persecuted believers in Jerusalem. He urges them to sow "bountifully," noting, "God loveth a cheerful giver."

READ:
2 Corinthians 6–9

Today's Date: _____

MY PRAYER FOR TODAY: ....
....
....

MY TAKEAWAY FROM
TODAY'S READING:

....
....
....
....
....
....

*Know
Your Bible:*

Paul warns the Corinthians
against false teachers, re-
minding them of his sufferings
on their behalf and describing
a vision of heaven that God
gave him.

READ:
2 Corinthians 10–13

Today's Date: _____

MY PRAYER FOR TODAY: ....
....
....

*Know
Your Bible:*

People are made right with
God not by their good works,
but by faith in Jesus Christ.
The spiritual life results in
"fruit" such as love, joy, peace,
patience, and gentleness.

READ:
Galatians 1–6

MY TAKEAWAY FROM
TODAY'S READING:

....
....
....
....
....
....

DAY 345

Today's Date: _____

MY PRAYER FOR TODAY: ....
....
....

Know Your Bible:

In Jesus Christ, Jews and Gentiles become one. Putting on "the new man," believers "walk in love" and wear the "whole armour of God" to stand against satanic attacks.

READ:
Ephesians 1–6

MY TAKEAWAY FROM TODAY'S READING:

....
....
....
....
....
....

DAY 346

Today's Date: _____

MY PRAYER FOR TODAY: ....
....
....

MY TAKEAWAY FROM TODAY'S READING:

....
....
....
....
....
....

Know Your Bible:

Christians should always "rejoice in the Lord," trading anxiety for "prayer and supplication with thanksgiving." God's peace will result.

READ:
Philippians 1–4

Today's Date: _____   DAY 347

MY PRAYER FOR TODAY: ....
....
....

MY TAKEAWAY FROM
TODAY'S READING:

....
....
....
....
....
....

Know Your Bible:

Jesus is "the image of the invisible God," in whom "dwelleth all the fulness of the godhead bodily." Raised with Him, believers should set their minds on heavenly things.

READ:
Colossians 1–4

Today's Date: _____   DAY 348

MY PRAYER FOR TODAY: ....
....
....

Know Your Bible:

While awaiting Jesus' return, every Christian should "possess his vessel in sanctification and honour." In time, Jesus will avenge His people of their persecutors.

READ:
1 Thessalonians 1–5;
2 Thessalonians 1–3

MY TAKEAWAY FROM
TODAY'S READING:

....
....
....
....
....
....

Today's Date: _____

MY PRAYER FOR TODAY: ....
....
....

Know Your Bible:

The apostle Paul tells young Timothy how to lead the church. "Take heed unto thyself, and unto thy doctrine. . . for in doing this thou shalt both save thyself, and them that hear thee."

READ:
1 Timothy 1–6

MY TAKEAWAY FROM TODAY'S READING:

....
....
....
....
....
....

Today's Date: _____

MY PRAYER FOR TODAY: ....
....
....

MY TAKEAWAY FROM TODAY'S READING:

....
....
....
....
....
....

Know Your Bible:

Two other "pastoral letters" share Paul's guidance. Timothy is to "endure hardness, as a good soldier of Jesus"; Titus, to "speak, and exhort, and rebuke with all authority."

READ:
2 Timothy 1–4;
Titus 1–3

Today's Date: _____

MY PRAYER FOR TODAY: ....
....
....

MY TAKEAWAY FROM
TODAY'S READING:

....
....
....
....
....
....

*Know
Your Bible:*

Philemon is urged to embrace
his runaway slave who became
a Christian. Hebrews shows
how Jesus and faith in Him are
superior to the Old Testament
Jewish experience.

READ:
Philemon;
Hebrews 1–6

Today's Date: _____

MY PRAYER FOR TODAY: ....
....
....

*Know
Your Bible:*

Old Testament law was just
a "shadow of good things to
come." Jesus, by shedding His
perfect blood on the cross,
"put away sin by the sacrifice
of himself."

READ:
Hebrews 7–10

MY TAKEAWAY FROM
TODAY'S READING:

....
....
....
....
....
....

DAY 353
Today's Date: _____

MY PRAYER FOR TODAY: ....
....
....

Know Your Bible:

Old Testament heroes such as Noah, Abraham, and Moses obeyed God by faith, just as Christians do. We now "offer the sacrifice of praise to God continually."

READ:
Hebrews 11–13

MY TAKEAWAY FROM TODAY'S READING:
....
....
....
....
....
....

DAY 354
Today's Date: _____

MY PRAYER FOR TODAY: ....
....
....

MY TAKEAWAY FROM TODAY'S READING:
....
....
....
....
....
....

Know Your Bible:

True Christian faith produces good works, such as caring for the poor. If we "draw nigh to God," He will draw near to us.

READ:
James 1–5

Today's Date: _____

MY PRAYER FOR TODAY: ....

....

MY TAKEAWAY FROM TODAY'S READING:

....

....

....

....

....

....

Know Your Bible:

Trials are temporary, but salvation is eternal. With "the end of all things" nearing, Christians should live wisely and prayerfully.

READ:
1 Peter 1–5

Today's Date: _____

MY PRAYER FOR TODAY: ....

....

Know Your Bible:

Beware of false teachers, who bring in "damnable heresies, even denying the Lord that bought them." Believers should grow in grace and their knowledge of Jesus.

READ:
2 Peter 1–3

MY TAKEAWAY FROM TODAY'S READING:

....

....

....

....

....

....

DAY 357

Today's Date: _____

MY PRAYER FOR TODAY: ....
....
....

Know Your Bible:

Christians have been lavishly loved by God and should therefore love each other. They are not to love "the things that are in the world."

READ:
1 John 1–5

MY TAKEAWAY FROM TODAY'S READING:
....
....
....
....
....
....

DAY 358

Today's Date: _____

MY PRAYER FOR TODAY: ....
....
....

MY TAKEAWAY FROM TODAY'S READING:
....
....
....
....
....
....

Know Your Bible:

John urges Christians to shun false teachers; Jude calls believers to "contend for the faith that was once delivered unto the saints."

READ:
2 John; 3 John; Jude

Today's Date: _____ DAY 359

MY PRAYER FOR TODAY: ....
....
....

MY TAKEAWAY FROM
TODAY'S READING:

....
....
....
....
....
....

Know Your Bible:

Jesus gives John messages for seven churches of Asia Minor. They are urged to hold fast their faith, repent of their sins, or—as with the Ephesians— remember "thy first love."

READ:
Revelation 1–3

Today's Date: _____ DAY 360

MY PRAYER FOR TODAY: ....
....
....

Know Your Bible:

John sees into heaven's throne room, where a seven-sealed scroll is opened by Jesus, looking like "a Lamb as it had been slain." Each seal unleashes God's wrath on the earth.

READ:
Revelation 4–6

MY TAKEAWAY FROM
TODAY'S READING:

....
....
....
....
....
....

DAY 361

Today's Date: _____

MY PRAYER FOR TODAY: ....
....
....

Know Your Bible:

When the final seal is broken, seven trumpets announce additional "woes" on the earth. Despite death and destruction, survivors "repented not" of their idolatry and evil.

READ:
Revelation 7–10

MY TAKEAWAY FROM TODAY'S READING:

....
....
....
....
....
....

DAY 362

Today's Date: _____

MY PRAYER FOR TODAY: ....
....
....

MY TAKEAWAY FROM TODAY'S READING:

....
....
....
....
....
....

Know Your Bible:

A dragon and a beast arise to oppose and blaspheme God, leading people into false worship. Those who refuse to worship the beast, identified by the number 666, are killed.

READ:
Revelation 11–13

Today's Date: _____

MY PRAYER FOR TODAY: ....

....

....

MY TAKEAWAY FROM TODAY'S READING:

....

....

....

....

....

....

Know Your Bible:

A "Lamb" appears on Mount Zion; an angel begins "the harvest of the earth"; and seven vials of wrath are poured out. Armies gather for battle at Armageddon.

READ:
Revelation 14–16

Today's Date: _____

MY PRAYER FOR TODAY: ....

....

....

Know Your Bible:

"Babylon the Great," which rules over the kings of earth, is destroyed, and God's people are avenged. Jesus returns to earth to destroy the beast and his armies.

READ:
Revelation 17–19

MY TAKEAWAY FROM TODAY'S READING:

....

....

....

....

....

....

Today's Date: _____

MY PRAYER FOR TODAY: ....
....
....

Know Your Bible:

Satan is cast into the lake of fire; God judges human beings either to eternal life or destruction; and "the holy city, new Jerusalem" descends from heaven to a restored earth.

READ:
Revelation 20–22

MY TAKEAWAY FROM TODAY'S READING:

....
....
....
....
....
....

THE PRAYER MAP. . .
for the Whole Family

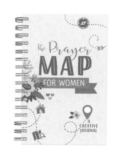

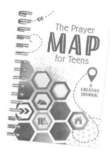

The Prayer Map for Men
978-1-64352-438-2

The Prayer Map for Women
978-1-68322-557-7

The Prayer Map for Girls
978-1-68322-559-1

The Prayer Map for Boys
978-1-68322-558-4

The Prayer Map for Teens
978-1-68322-556-0

This series of purposeful prayer journals is a fun and creative way to more fully experience the power of prayer! Each inspiring journal page guides you to write out thoughts, ideas, and lists. . .which then creates a specific "map" for you to follow as you talk to God.

Spiral Bound / $7.99

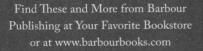